DANCE WORLD

by
JOHN WILLIS

1966

Volume 1

CROWN PUBLISHERS, INC.
New York

To

RUTH ST. DENIS

and

TED SHAWN

. . . whose dedication to their art brought recognition to creative dancers in the United States and influenced theatre dance throughout the world

Vaslav Nijinsky—1937

Ruth St. Denis in "The Peacock"—1933

Anna Pavlova—1924

Ted Shawn in "Cosmic Dance Of Seva"—1926

4

THE PAST IN REVIEW

CONTENTS

John Willis, Editor

Harold Stephens, Assistant Editor

Advisers: Jack Moore, William Como

Staff: Jane Monroe, Charlotte Rahaim, Lucy Williams

Staff Photographers: Louis Mélançon, Van Williams

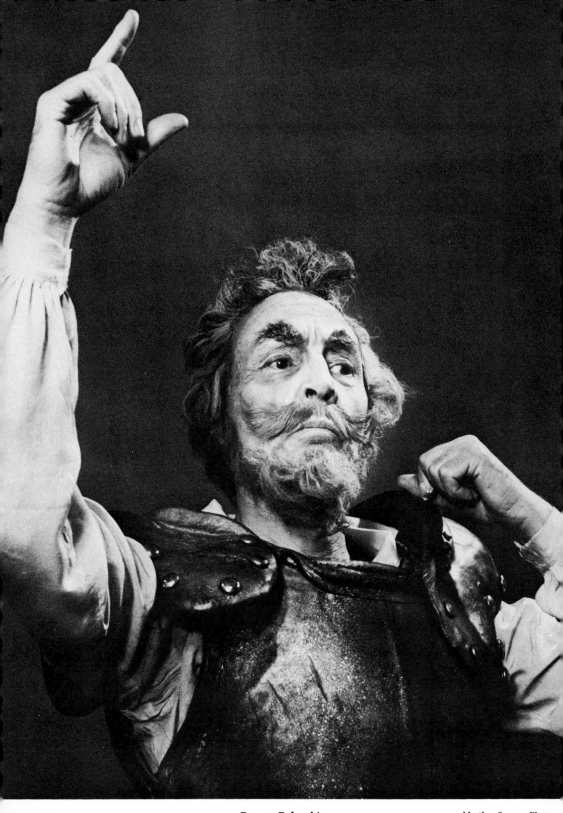

George Balanchine
as
Don Quixote

NEW YORK STATE THEATER

Opened Tuesday, June 1, 1965.*
The City Center of Music and Drama,
Inc. (Jean Dalrymple, Director) presents
The New York City Ballet in:

DON QUIXOTE

A Ballet in three acts; Choreographed by
George Balanchine; Music by Nicolas Nabokov;
Commissioned by the New York City Ballet;
Scenery, Costumes, and Lighting, Esteban
Frances; Masks and Armor, Lawrence Vlady;
Giant, Kermit Love, Peter Sahlin; Conductors,
Robert Irving, Hugo Fiorato.

CAST

PROLOGUE:
Don Quixote _____ George Balanchine
              (opening night only), Richard Rapp
Fantasies _____ Judith Fugate, Peter Allner,
      George D'Amboise, Alexander Foster,
      Peter Haig, Timothy Maduro
Dulcinea _____ Suzanne Farrell

ACT I:
Sancho Panza _____ Deni Lamont
A Peasant _____ Shaun O'Brien
A Boy _____ Stephen Guagenti
Slaves _____ George Diaz, Richard Lichter,
      Frances Sackett, Bojan Spassoff,
      Edgar Valdez, Stephen Varjan
Guards _____ Robert Maiorano, Larry O'Brien
Market Vendors _____ Ericca Goodman,
              Karen Morell, Virginia Stuart
Waitresses _____ Gail Kachadurian,
              Margaret Wood
Cafe Proprietor _____ Shaun O'Brien
Townspeople ____ Karen Batizi, Diane Bradshaw,
      Marjorie Bresler, Elaine Comsudi, Gail
      Crisa, Suzanne Erlon, Penelope Gates,
      Janet Greschler, Susan Hendl, Lise Ken-
      niff, Ruth Ann King, Delia Peters, Susan
      Pillersdorf, Bettijane Sills, Lynne Stet-
      son, Karin von Aroldingen, Anthony
      Blum, Truman Finney, John Prinz,
      David Richardson, Robert Rodham,
      Earle Sieveling, Michael Steele, Kent
      Stowell
Dead Poet _____ Paul Sackett
His Friend _____ Conrad Ludlow
Pall Bearers _____ Edgar Valdez, Stephen Varjan
Marcela _____ Suzanne Farrell
Policemen _____ Roger Peterson, Roger Pietrucha
Organ Grinder _____ Robert Maiorano
Puppeteer _____ Michael Arshansky
Puppets:
    Saracens _____ Alexander Stetson, Susan
      Linfield, Melissa MacFarlane, Jann Meri
      Trambert, Ellen Weisbarth
Christian Girl _____ ____ Judith Fugate
Christian Boy _____ Jean Pierre Froelich
Palace Guards ____ George Diaz, Richard Lichter,
              Frances Sackett, Bojan Spassoff
Ladies in Waiting _____ Leslie Ruchala,
              Ellen Shire
Gentlemen in Waiting _____ Roland Vazquez,
              William Weslow
The Duke _____ Nicholas Magallanes
The Duchess _____ Jillana

ACT II:
Ladies and Gentlemen of the
    Court _____ Marjorie Bresler, Elaine Comsudi,
      Penelope Gates, Gail Kachadurian, Lise
      Kenniff, Ruth Ann King, Teena Mc-
      Connell, Lynne Stetson, Truman Finney,
      Robert Maiorano, Larry O'Brien, Shaun
      O'Brien, Roger Peterson, Roger Pie-
      trucha, David Richardson, Michael Steele
Major Domo _____ Michael Arshansky
Merlin _____ Francisco Moncion
Divertissements:
    Rigaudon Flamenco _____ Gloria Govrin,
              Arthur Mitchell
    Danza de la Caccia _____ Patricia Neary,
              Conrad Ludlow, Kent Stowell
    Pas de deux Mauresque _____ Suki Schorer,
              John Prinz
    Courante Sicilienne _____ Sara Leland,
      Kay Mazzo, Carol Sumner, Frank Oh-
      man, Robert Rodham, Earle Sieveling
    Ritornel ____ Patricia McBride, Colleen Neary

**George Balanchine
as Don Quixote**

Martha Swope Photo

ACT III:
Knight of The Silver Moon ____ Conrad Ludlow
Maidens _____ Marnee Morris, Mimi Paul, Karen
      Batizi, Diane Bradshaw, Marjorie Bresler,
      Gail Crisa, Rosemary Dunleavy, Suzanne
      Erlon, Ericca Goodman, Janet Greschler,
      Susan Hendl, Ruth Ann King, Kay Mazzo,
      Karen Morell, Delia Peters, Susan Pillers-
      dorf, Lynne Stetson, Margaret Wood
Cavaliers _____ Anthony Blum, Frank Ohman
    Variation I _____ Mimi Paul
    Variation II _____ Marnee Morris
    Variation III _____ Anthony Blum
    Variation IV _____ Suzanne Farrell
Merlin _____ Francisco Moncion
Night Spirit _____ Gloria Govrin
Bearers _____ Larry O'Brien, Shaun O'Brien,
         David Richardson, Michael Steele
Housekeeper _____ Karin von Aroldingen
Priest _____ Michael Arshansky

General Manager: Betty Cage
Company Manager: Zelda Dorfman
Press: Virginia Donaldson, Doris Luhrs
Stage Managers: Ronald Bates, Kevin Tyler,
Mel Schierman

* Closed June 5, 1965. (10 performances)

Richard Rapp, Suzanne Farrell
Above: George Balanchine

Deni Lamont (on floor), Richard Rapp (on horse)
Above: George Balanchine

New York City Ballet in "Don Quixote"

Front: Suki Schorer, John Prinz
Rear: Jillana, Nicholas Magallanes
New York City Ballet in "Don Quixote"

Kent Stowell, Patricia Neary, Conrad Ludlow
Above: Suzanne Farrell

9

Martha Swope Photo

Fred Fehl Photo

Arthur Mitchell, also above with
Edward Villella, Melissa Hayden

NEW YORK STATE THEATER

Opened Wednesday, June 9, 1965.°
The City Center of Music and Drama
(Jean Dalrymple, Director) presents the
New York City Ballet in:

A MIDSUMMER NIGHT'S DREAM

Music, Felix Mendelssohn; Choreography,
George Balanchine; Costumes, Karinska; Scenery, David Hays; Conductor, Robert Irving;
General Director, Lincoln Kirstein; Ballet Masters, George Balanchine, John Taras; Associate Ballet Mistress, Una Kai; Assistant Ballet
Mistress, Francia Russell.

CAST

SINGERS: Veronica Tyler, Malka Schwarz,
Betty Baisch, Barbara Beaman, Helen Guile,
Mitzi Wilson

ACT I: A forest near Athens, on Midsummer
Eve

Butterflies .... Suki Schorer, Delia Peters,
Bail Crisa, Karen Morell, Susan Pillersdorf,
Margaret Wood, Sylvia Blaustein, Diahann
Brown, Naomi Cohn, Meg Gordon, Ulyana
Maystrenko, Joan Reibman, Kobie Thakar
Puck .... Arthur Mitchell
Helena .... Jillana, Mimi Paul
Oberon .... Edward Villella
Oberon's Pages .... Gelsey Kirkland,
Susan Rollins, Katherine Voinoff,
Catherine Wheeler
Titania .... Melissa Hayden, Jillana,
Suzanne Farrell
Titania's Cavalier .... Conrad Ludlow,
Anthony Blum
Titania's Page .... Lynette Henry
Bottom .... Richard Rapp
Bottom's Companions .... Shaun O'Brien,
Larry O'Brien, Frank Ohman
Theseus .... Francisco Moncion
Courtiers to Theseus ...... Wilhelm Burmann,
Alfonso Cata, Roger Peterson,
Roger Pietrucha
Hermia .... Patricia McBride,
Sara Leland
Lysander .... Nicholas Magallanes
Demetrius .... Roland Vazquez
Titania's Retinue .... Marjorie Bresler,
Elaine Comsudi, Penelope Gates, Susan
Hendl, Ruth Ann King, Kay Mazzo, Teena
McConnell, Leslie Ruchala, Ellen Shire,
Bettijane Sills, Lynne Stetson, Karin von
Aroldingen
Oberon's Kingdom:
Butterflies and Fairies.........Vicki Bromberg,
Nina Bzorad, Daria Flessas, Susan Friedman,
Julia Hays, Wendy Kahn, Barbara Manilla,
Marcelle Meyer, Catherine Neuman, Con-
stance Rosenberg, Elizabeth Rosenthal, Gina
Roose, Karen Strand, Stephanie Petrillo,
Devon Mathews, Wendy Wells
Hippolyta .... Gloria Govrin, Patricia Neary
Hippolyta's Hounds .... Diane Bradshaw,
Suzanne Erlon, Ericca Goodman, Janet
Greschler, Susan Hendl, Linda MacArthur

ACT II: At the court of Theseus in Athens
for wedding ceremony

Courtiers .... Karen Batizi, Marjorie Bresler,
Elaine Comsudi, Diane Bradshaw, Gail Crisa,
Suzanne Erlon, Penelope Gates, Janet
Greschler, Gail Kachadurian, Ruth Ann King,
Karen Morell, Linda MacArthur, Susan
Hendl, Ericca Goodman, Delia Peters, Susan
Pillersdorf, Lynne Stetson, Margaret Wood,
Truman Finney, Alfonso Cata, Wilhelm
Burmann, Roger Peterson, Roger Pietrucha,
John Prinz, Larry O'Brien, David Richardson
Divertissement .... Allegra Kent, Jacques
D'Amboise with Rosemary Dunleavy, Kay
Mazzo, Marnee Morris, Suki Schorer, Betti-
jane Sills, Carol Sumner, Deni Lamont,
Richard Rapp, Robert Rodham, Frank
Ohman, Earle Sieveling, William Weslow

General Manager: Betty Cage
Assistant Manager: Edward Bigelow
Company Manager: Zelda Dorfman
Press: Virginia Donaldson, Doris Luhrs
Stage Managers: Roland Bates,
Kevin Tyler, Mel Schierman

° Closed Saturday, June 12, 1965.
(6 performances)

Melissa Hayden, Richard Rapp   Edward Villella, Suzanne Farrell
Top: (C) Melissa Hayden, Conrad Ludlow

Melissa Hayden, Jacques D'Amboise in "Swan Lake"
Above: Maria Tallchief, Arthur Mitchell
in "Piege De Lumiere"

Edward Villella, Patricia McBride in "Harlequinade"
Above: Allegra Kent in "La Sonnambula"

NEW YORK STATE THEATER

Opened Thursday, Sept. 23, 1965.°
The City Center of Music and Drama, Inc.
(Jean Dalrymple, Director) presents:

NEW YORK CITY BALLET

General Director, Lincoln Kirstein; Ballet
Masters, George Balanchine, John Taras; Asso-
ciate Ballet Mistress, Una Kai; Assistant Ballet
Mistress, Francia Russell; Costumes, Karinska;
NYC Ballet Orchestra Principal Conductor,
Robert Irving; Associate Conductor, Hugo
Fiorato.

PRINCIPAL DANCERS

Jacques D'Amboise, Melissa Hayden, Jillana,
Allegra Kent, Conrad Ludlow, Nicholas Magal-
lanes, Patricia McBride, Arthur Mitchell, Fran-
cisco Moncion, Andre Prokovsky, Maria Tall-
chief, Violette Verdy, Edward Villella, Patricia
Wilde, Anthony Blum, Suzanne Farrell, Gloria
Govrin, Deni Lamont, Sara Leland, Patricia
Neary, Mimi Paul, Richard Rapp, Robert Rod-
ham, Suki Schorer, Earle Sieveling, Victoria
Simon, Kent Stowell, Carol Sumner, Roland
Vazquez, William Weslow, Karin von Arolding-
en, Karen Barizi, Diane Bradshaw, Marjorie
Bresler, Elaine Comsudi, Gail Crisa, James
DeBolt, Rosemary Dunleavy, Suzanne Erlon,
Truman Finney, Penelope Gates, Ericca Good-
man, Janet Greschler, Susan Hendl, Gail Ka-
chadurian, Lise Kenniff, Ruth Ann King, Robert
Maiorano, Kay Mazzo, Teena McConnell, Karen
Morell, Marnee Morris, Larry O'Brien, Shaun
O'Brien, Frank Ohman, Delia Peters, Roger
Peterson, Roger Pietrucha, Susan Pillersdorf,
John Prinz, David Richardson, Leslie Ruchala,
Ellen Shire, Bettijane Sills, Michael Steele,
Lynne Stetson, Virginia Stuart, Margaret Wood

REPERTOIRE

Don Quixote, Raymonda Variations, Taran-
tella, Stars and Stripes, Agon, Irish Fantasy,
Liebeslieder Walzer, Harlequinade, La Valse,
Swan Lake, Allegro Brillante, Meditation, Sym-
phony In C, Firebird, Concerto Barocco, Prod-
igal Son, Pas De Deux and Divertissement,
Scotch Symphony, Four Temperaments, Con
Amore, Piege De Lumiere, Ballet Imperial,
Episodes, La Sonnambula, Interplay, Bugaku,
Monumentum Pro Gesualdo, Donizetti Varia-
tions, Movements For Piano and Orchestra.

General Manager: Betty Cage
Assistant Manager: Edward Bigelow
Company Manager: Zelda Dorfman
Press: Virginia Donaldson, Doris Luhrs
Stage Managers: Donald Bates, Kevin Tyler

° Opening production of "Don Quixote" was
given 15 performances through Sunday, Oct.
3, 1965. Repertory opened Tuesday, Oct. 5
and closed Sunday, Oct. 31, 1965, after 38
performances.

Martha Swope Photos

Patricia McBride, Edward Villella
in "Pas De Deux"

Nicholas Magallanes, Violette Verdy
in "Liebeslieder Walzer"
Above: Maria Tallchief, Francisco Moncion in "Firebird" 13

William Weslow, Patricia Neary, Richard Rapp
in "Scotch Symphony"
Above: "Agon"
New York City Ballet

Margrethe Schanne
in
"La Sylphide"
Royal Danish Ballet

Opened Tuesday, November 23, 1965.°
S. Hurok presents under the patronage
of His Majesty King Frederik IX of
Denmark:

THE ROYAL DANISH BALLET

General Administrator, Henning A. Brond-
sted; General Manager, Jens Louis Petersen;
Ballet Director, Niels Bjorn Larsen; Conductors,
Poul Jorgensen, Robert Blot, Arthur Lief.

GUEST ARTISTS: Erik Bruhn, Flemming
Flindt, Margrethe Schanne
SOLO DANCERS: Ruth Andersen, Verner
Andersen, Fredbjorn Bjornsson, Eske Holm,
Svend Erik Jensen, Niels Kehlet, Henning Kron-
stam, Anna Laerkesen, Jorn Madsen, Margrethe
Schanne, Frank Schaufuss, Kirsten Simone,
Solveig Ostergaard
DANCERS: Arne Bech, Jens Brenaa, Lotte
Cornelius-Knudsen, Lise la Cour, Elisabeth
Enevoldsen, Ole Fatum, Liselotte Frimann,
Tommy Frishoi, Vivi Gelker, Ingrid Glinde-
mann, Flemming Halby, Nina Herlov, Mette
Honningen, Inge Jensen, Lillian Jensen, Ulla
Skow Jensen, Vita Johansen, Annelise Johnsen,
Iben Kehlet, Mona Kiil, Frantz Kjaerulff, Eva
Kloborg, Hans Jacob Kolgaard, Dinna Bjorn
Larsen, Peter Martins, Kjeld Noack, Inge Olaf-
sen, Annemette Petersen, Aage Poulsen, Benny
Poulsen, Lizzie Rode, Vibeke Roland, Mogens
Rud, Flemming Ryberg, Viveka Segerskog, Ole
Suhr, Palle Sorensen, Anne Marie Vessel, Anne-
mari Vingaard, Arlette Weinrich, Tage Wendt
REPERTOIRE: "Romeo and Juliet," "Fan-
fare," "Carmen," "Napoli," "Coppelia," "Kon-
servatoriet," "Miss Julie," "Whims Of Cupid,"
"The Private Lesson," "La Sylphide," "Moon
Reindeer."

Company Manager: Edward A. Perper
Press: Martin Feinstein, Michael Sweeley,
Edward Parkinson
Stage Managers: Poul Vessel,
Knud Hogenhaven

° Closed Sunday, December 19, 1965.
(32 performances)

Mydtskov Photos

Eske Holm, Anna Laerkesen
in "Romeo and Juliet"

Anna Laerkesen, Lillian Jensen
in "Romeo and Juliet"
Above: Kirsten Simone, Henning Kronstam
in "Romeo and Juliet"

Niels Kehlet in "Coppelia"
Above: Kirsten Simone, Erik Bruhn
in "Carmen"

Solveig Ostergaard, Ruth Andersen
in "Napoli"

Verner Andersen, Mette Honnigen
in "Moon Reindeer"
Above: Kirsten Simone, Henning Kronstam
in "La Sylphide"

18   Royal Danish Ballet

Inge Olafsen (C) in "Fanfare"
Above: Ruth Andersen, Solveig Ostergaard
in "Konservatoriet"
Top: (C) Arlette Weinreich, Fredbjorn Bjornsson
in "Napoli"

Jorn Madsen in "La Sylphide"
Above: Henning Kronstam
in "The Lesson"

Vivi Gelker, Frank Schaufuss
in "Miss Julie"
Above: Solveig Ostergaard, Niels Kehlet
in "Coppelia"

Mydtskov Photo

Erik Bruhn, Kirsten Simone
in
"Miss Julie"
Royal Danish Ballet

Opened Friday, December 24, 1965.°
The City Center of Music and Drama
(Jean Dalrymple, Director) presents the
New York City Ballet in:

THE NUTCRACKER

Based on E.T.A. Hoffman's "The Nutcracker
and The Mouse King;" Music, P. Tschaikovsky;
Choreography, George Balanchine; Scenery
and Lighting, Rouben Ter-Arutunian; Costumes,
Karinska; Conductors, Robert Irving, Hugo
Fiorato; Violin Soloist, Marilyn Wright; Children from The School of American Ballet;
General Director, Lincoln Kirstein; Ballet Masters, George Balanchine, John Taras; Associate
Ballet Mistress, Una Kai; Assistant Ballet Mistress, Francia Russell.

CAST

Dr. Stahlbaum _____ Roland Vazquez
Frau Stahlbaum _____ Penelope Gates
Their Children:
 Marie _____ Judith Fugate, Paige Pedersen
 Fritz _ David Wallach, Catherine Neuman
The Maid _____ Johnna Kirkland
The Guests:
 Parents ____ Marjorie Bresler, Elaine Comsudi,
  Ruth Ann King, Lynne Stetson, Larry
  O'Brien, Roger Peterson, Roger Pietrucha,
  Michael Steele
 Children ____ Vicki Bromberg, Susan Linfield,
  Melissa MacFarlane, Deborah Marx, Debra
  Matthews, Toby Pierce, Constance Rosenberg, Barbara Sarafian, Phillip Terence,
  Susanna Thomas, Jann-Meri Trambert,
  Nina Brzorad, Catherine Clymer, Laura
  Flagg, Darria Flessas, Martha Gehman,
  Julia Hays, Mimi Lasker, Devon Mathews,
  Robbie Rodkin, Leslie Urdang, Ellen
  Weisbarth
Grandparents _____ Giselle Roberge, John Prinz
Herr Drosselmeier _____ Shaun O'Brien
His Nephew
 (The Nutcracker) _____ Michael Gaines,
   Jean-Pierre Frolich
Harlequin and Columbine ____ Karen Morell,
   Margeret Wood
Soldier _____ William Weslow
Mouse King _____ Michael Steele
Mice _____ Wilhelm Burmann, Alfonso Cata,
 Paul Mejia, Robert Maiorano, Larry O'Brien,
 Roger Peterson, Roger Pietrucha, John Prinz
Soldiers _____ Sophie Arnold, Debra Axelson,
 Jennifer Block, Giselle Calderon, Carla Corwin, Juliana Frosch, Edith Geringer, Barbara
 Gladston, Lisa Klein, Wendy Littlefield,
 Nancy Manus, Katherine McCarthy, Cynthia
 Mims, Chary Penner, Stephanie Petrillo, Lisa
 Rasmussen, Nancy Simon, Cassandra Smith,
 Leslie Weiss, Janet Arons, Leslie Alters,
 Susan Conneally, Susan Drogin, Nicole Edell,
 Lynette Henry, Joanne Hochberg, Wendy
 Kahn, Gina Kovarsky, Abigail Laufer, Madeleine Lee, Robin MacDonald, Vicky Marsen,
 Kim Richardson, Elizabeth Rosenthal, Martha
 Rosenthal, Landis Smith, Kathleen Waite,
 Hilda Wylie
The Snowflakes _____ Karin von Aroldingen,
 Karen Batizi, Diane Bradshaw, Marjorie
 Bresler, Elaine Comsudi, Gail Crisa, Rosemary
 Dunleavy, Suzanne Erlon, Janet Greschler,
 Susan Hendl, Gail Kachadurian, Linda MacArthur, Jennifer Nairn-Smith, Delia Peters,
 Susan Pillersdorf, Lynne Stetson
The Sugar Plum Fairy _____ Patricia McBride,
   Suzanne Farrell, Mimi Paul,
   Allegra Kent, Melissa Hayden
The Little Princess _____ Judith Fugate,
   Paige Pedersen
The Little Prince _____ Michael Gaines,
   Jean-Pierre Frolich
Angels _____ Debra Axelson, Jennifer Block,
 Carla Corwin, Juliana Frosch, Barbara Gladson, Edith Geringer, Lisa Klein, Nancy
 Manus, Katherine McCarthy, Chary Penner,
 Cassandra Smith, Leslie Weiss, Susan Drogin,
 Nicole Edell, Laura Flagg, Lynette Henry,
 Joanne Hochberg, Madeleine Lee, Vicky
 Marsen, Kim Richardson, Elizabeth Rosenthal, Martha Rosenthal, Leslie Urdang,
 Hilda Wylie
Hot Chocolate _____ Marnee Morris,
 John Prinz, Sara Leland, Janet Greschler,
 Johnna Kirkland, Nanette Reedy, Giselle
 Roberge, Robert Maiorano, Roger Peterson,
 Roger Pietrucha, Michael Steele
Tea _____ Deni Lamont, Karen Morell,
   Margaret Wood

Martha Swope Photo

"The Nutcracker"

Candy Canes _____ Richard Rapp,
 Sylvia Blaustein, Naomi Cohn, Clarisse
 Giffler, Katherine Goldrosen, Alice Patelson,
 Lisa Rasmussen, Joan Reibman, Kobie Thakar,
 Elise Flagg, Nanette Glushak, Ellen Goldschlag, Gelsey Kirkland, Ulyana Maystrenko,
 Marcelle Meyer, Katherine Voinoff, Catherine
 Wheeler
Marzipan Shepherdesses _____ Suki Schorer,
 Carol Sumner, Rosemary Dunleavy, Kay
 Mazzo, Delia Peters, Virginia Stuart
Mother Ginger and her
 polichinelles _____ David Richardson,
 Vicki Bromberg, Susan Linfield, Deborah
 Marx, Melissa MacFarlane, Debra Matthews,
 Constance Rosenberg, Susanna Thomas,
 Jann-Meri Trambert, Nina Brzorad, Diahann
 Brown, Catherine Clymer, Darria Flessas,
 Martha Gehman, Devon Mathews, Catherine
 Neuman, Ellen Weisbarth
Dewdrop ____ _____ Patricia McBride,
 Suzanne Farrell, Patricia Neary, Mimi Paul,
 Marnee Morris, Gloria Govrin
Flowers _____ Teena McConnell, Bettijane
 Sills, Karen Batizi, Diane Bradshaw, Marjorie Bresler, Elaine Comsudi, Suzanne Erlon,
 Penelope Gates, Susan Hendl, Gail Kachadurian, Linda MacArthur, Jennifer Nairn-Smith, Donna Sackett, Lynne Stetson
The Sugar Plum Fairy
 and her Cavalier _____ Suzanne Farrell
 and Jacques D'Amboise, Patricia McBride
 and Edward Villella, Allegra Kent and
 Conrad Ludlow, Mimi Paul and Anthony
 Blum, Melissa Hayden and Andre Prokovsky

A Classic Ballet in two acts, four scenes
and prologue.

General Manager: Betty Cage
Company Manager: Zelda Dorfman
Press: Doris Luhrs
Stage Managers: Roland Bates, Kevin Tyler

° Closed Sunday, January 16, 1966, after a
limited engagement of 32 performances.

Scenes from "The Nutcracker"   Edward Villella
New York City Ballet

Scenes from "The Nutcracker"
New York City Ballet

Martha Swope and Fred Fehl Photos

23

Antony Tudor

Opened Tuesday, January 18, 1966.°
Ballet Theatre Foundation, Inc. (Harold Taylor, President) presents:

AMERICAN BALLET THEATRE

Lucia Chase and Oliver Smith, Directors; Assistant to the Directors, John Kriza; Regisseur, Dimitri Romanoff; Ballet Master, Enrique Martinez; Conductor, Walter Hagen; Guest Conductor, Kenneth Schermerhorn.

PRINCIPAL DANCERS: Lupe Serrano, Royes Fernandez, Toni Lander, Scott Douglas, John Kriza, Ruth Ann Koesun, Bruce Marks, Sallie Wilson, Eleanor D'Antuono, Gayle Young

GUEST ARTISTS: Carmen deLavallade, Mary Hinkson

DANCERS: Susan Borree, Veronika Mlakar, Basil Thompson, Paul Sutherland, Janet Mitchell, Joseph Carow, Karen Krych, Ted Kivitt, Victoria Leigh, Edward Verso, Jeanne Armin, William Glassman, Judith Lerner, Eliot Feld, Erin Martin, Tom Adair, Diane Anthony, Amy Blaisdell, Karena Brock, Susan Casey, Camille Crosby, Ellen Everett, Cynthia Gregory, Virginia Griffee, Judi Griffler, Alaine Haubert, Reese Haworth, Terry Hilton, Rosamond Lynn, Ray Morgan, Gilda Mullett, Alexandra Nadal, Paul Nickel, Terry Orr, Marcos Peredes, Christine Sarry, Gretchen Schumacher, Rosanna Seravalli, John Sowinski, Burton Taylor, Carol Todd, Diana Weber, Kasana Wojcik, Richard Zelens

REPERTOIRE: Theme and Variations, Dark Elegies, Jardin Aux Lilas, The Wind In The Mountains, The Combat, The Four Marys, Pillar of Fire, Balladen Der Liebe, Grand Pas-Glazounov, Fall River Legend, Sargasso, La Fille Mal Gardee, Billy The Kid, Kontraste, Ricercare, Etudes, Peter and The Wolf, Giselle, Les Sylphides, Swan Lake, Interplay, Pas De Deux, Miss Julie, Les Noces, Esmeralda Pas De Deux, Fancy Free, Don Quixote Pas De Deux, Caprichos.

Production Manager: Daryl Dodson
Press: Samuel Lurie, Stanley F. Kaminsky
Stage Managers: Tom Porter,
Joseph Carow

° Closed Sunday, February 13, 1966.
(32 performances)

Jack Mitchell Photos

**Lupe Serrano, Royes Fernandez
in "Giselle"**

**Carmen de Lavallade, Judith Lerner
in "The Four Marys"
Above: Bruce Marks, Toni Lander
in "Miss Julie"**

25

Royes Fernandez, Toni Lander
in "La Sylphide"
Above: "La Sylphide". Top: "Billy The Kid"
American Ballet Theatre

Sallie Wilson in "Fall River Legend"
Above: "Les Noces"

Scott Douglas, Mary Hinkson
in "Ricercare"
Above: Sallie Wilson, Ellen Everett, Tom Adair
in "Pillar Of Fire"

American Ballet Theatre

"Etudes". Above: (L) Edward Verso, William Glassman, Eliot Feld, Ellen Everett
in "Fancy Free". (R) "Kontraste". Top: Lupe Serrano, Royes Fernandez
in "Theme and Variations"
American Ballet Theatre

Gayle Young, Sallie Wilson in "Swan Lake"
Above: "The Wind In The Mountains"
Top: Bruce Marks, Sallie Wilson in "Sargasso"

Toni Lander, Royes Fernandez
in "La Sylphide"
Top: Sallie Wilson (C) in "Les Noces"

American Ballet Theatre

NEW YORK STATE THEATER

Opened Tuesday, March 29, 1966.°
The New York City Center of Music
and Drama (Jean Dalrymple, Director)
presents in repertory:

NEW YORK CITY BALLET

General Director, Lincoln Kirstein; Ballet
Masters, George Balanchine, John Taras; Associate Ballet Mistress, Una Kai; Assistant
Ballet Mistress, Francia Russell; NYC Ballet
Orchestra Conductors, Robert Irving, Hugo
Fiorato; Costumes, Karinska.

COMPANY

PRINCIPAL DANCERS: Jacques D'Amboise,
Melissa Hayden, Jillana, Allegra Kent, Conrad
Ludlow, Nicholas Magallanes, Patricia McBride, Arthur Mitchell, Francisco Moncion,
Andre Prokovsky, Maria Tallchief, Violette
Verdy, Edward Villella, Patricia Wilde.

Anthony Blum, Suzanne Farrell, Gloria Govrin,
Deni Lamont, Sara Leland, Patricia Neary,
Mimi Paul, Richard Rapp, Robert Rodham,
Suki Schorer, Earle Sieveling, Victoria Simon,
Kent Stowell, Carol Sumner, Roland Vazquez,
William Weslow

Karin von Aroldingen, Karen Barizi, Diane
Bradshaw, Marjorie Bresler, Elaine Comsudi,
Gail Crisa, James DeBolt, Rosemary Dunleavy,
Suzanne Erlon, Truman Finney, Penelope Gates,
Ericca Goodman, Janet Greschler, Susan Hendl,
Gail Kachadurian, Lise Kenniff, Ruth Ann
King, Robert Maiorano, Kay Mazzo, Teena McConnell, Karen Morell, Marnee Morris, Larry
O'Brien, Frank Ohman, Delia Peters, Roger
Peterson, Roger Pietrucha, Susan Pillersdorf,
John Prinz, David Richardson, Leslie Ruchala,
Ellen Shire, Bettijane Sills, Michael Steele,
Lynne Stetson, Virginia Stuart, Margaret Wood.

REPERTOIRE

Scotch Symphony, Pas De Deux, The Cage,
La Valse, Serenade, Ebony Concerto, Tarantella, Prodigal Son, Raymonda Variations, Apollo, Stars and Stripes, Agon, Meditation, Harlequinade, Pas De Deux and Divertissement,
Allegro Brillante, La Valse, A Midsummer
Night's Dream, Bugaku, Afternoon Of A Faun,
Irish Fantasy, Donizetti Variations, Swan Lake,
Con Amore, Firebird, Serenade, Ballet Imperial, La Sonnambula, Divertimento No. 15,
Piege De Lumiere, Monumentum Pro Gesualdo,
Movements For Piano and Orchestra, Liebeslieder Walzer, Dim Lustre, Don Quixote.

PREMIERES: Variations (Music, Igor Stravinsky (Aldous Huxley Variation: 1965);
Choreography, George Balanchine), Summerspace (Music, Morton Feldman; Choreography,
Merce Cunningham; Scenery and Costumes,
Robert Rauschenberg); Brahms-Schoenberg
Quartet (Music, Johannes Brahms; Orchestrated
by Arnold Schoenberg in 1937; Choreography,
George Balanchine; Costumes, Karinska), Jeux
(Music, Achille-Claude Debussy; Choreography,
John Taras), La Guirlande De Campra (Music, based on theme of Andre Campra is series
of variations by Georges Auric, Arthur Honegger, Daniel Lesur, Alexis Roland-Manuel, Francis Poulenc, Henri Sauguet, and Germaine
Tailleferre; Choreography, John Taras).

General Manager: Betty Cage
Assistant Manager: Edward Bigelow
Company Manager: Zelda Dorfman
Press: Doris Luhrs
Stage Managers: Donald Bates, Kevin Tyler
° Closed Sunday, May 22, 1966 after 62 performances. "Don Quixote" was performed for
the final 14 performances.

Martha Swope Photos

"Variations"
30 Above: Edward Villella, Melissa Hayden, Allegra Kent
in "Jeux"

"Variations"
Above: Melissa Hayden, Edward Villella, Allegra Kent in "Jeux"
New York City Ballet

Scenes from "Summerspace"

Deni Lamont
Above: Kay Mazzo, Anthony Blum

New York City Ballet

Martha Swope Photos

Suzanne Farrell, Jacques D'Amboise
Above: (L) Edward Villella, Allegra Kent. (R) Kent Stowell, Patricia McBride
Scenes from "Brahms-Schoenberg Quartet"
New York City Ballet

Allegra Kent, Francisco Moncion
in "The Cage"
Above: (L) Mimi Paul, Arthur Mitchell
in "Bugaku"

Jacques D'Amboise, Allegra Kent
in "Afternoon Of A Faun"
Above: Melissa Hayden, Nicholas Magallanes
in "Allegro Brillante"
Top: "Stars and Stripes"

New York City Ballet

"Four Temperaments"
Above: Edward Villella, Patricia Neary
in "Prodigal Son"
Top: "Ballet Imperial"

Jillana, Nicholas Magallanes, Melissa Hayden
in "Serenade"

New York City Ballet

NEW YORK CITY CENTER

Opened Wednesday, November 17, 1965.°
New York City Center Drama Company
(Jean Dalrymple, Director) in association
with Ronald A. Wilford Associates, Inc.,
presents:

MARCEL MARCEAU
and his partner Pierre Verry
in a program of pantomimes

PART I: The Kite, The Man and His Boat,
The Magician, The Bureaucrats, The Cage,
Circus Performer, The Seven Deadly Sins,
Walking, Walking Against the Wind, The Stair-
case, The Sculptor, The Public Garden,
The Mask Maker, Youth, Maturity, Old Age
and Death.

PART II: BIP—goes to an Audition, as a
Matador, dreams he is Don Juan, as a Soldier,
goes traveling, in the Subway, as a Baby
Sitter, at a Society Party, as a Lion Tamer,
takes an Ocean Voyage, hunts Butterflies, plays
David and Goliath, the Street Musician, looks
for a job on New Year's Eve.

General Manager: Homer Poupart
Company Manager: John Trelfall
Administrative Director: Alain Mangel
Press: Herbert Breslin
Stage Managers: Louis Thomas,
Tennent McDaniel

Closed Sunday, December 12, 1965. (24
performances) United States tenth anniversary tour.

Lillian Libman Photos

Marcel Marceau

Antonio and Rosario

John Blomfield Photo

NEW YORK CITY CENTER
Opened Tuesday, January 4, 1966.°
S. Hurok presents:

ANTONIO
and
THE BALLETS DE MADRID

GUEST ARTIST, ROSARIO

Direction, Choreography, and Lighting by Antonio; Assistant Director, Juan Ayala; Musical Director, Silvio Masciarelli; Ballet Master, Dino Lucchetta.

DANCERS: Alicia Diaz, Paco Romero, Mariana, Angela Del Moral, Carmen Roche, Pastora Ruiz, Jose Antonio, Enrique Gutierrez, Angel Garcia, Luis Ardiz, Teo Santelmo, Dino Lucchetta, Fabian Alonzo, Paco Alonzo, Paloma Andia, Emilia Baylo, Carlos Fernandez, Luis Flores, Elena Gandia, Mary Nieves, Ricardo Monte, Lina Montes, Salvador Napolitano, Flora Navarrete, Julia Perez, Jesus Ramos, Conchita Vidal

SINGERS: Clara Maria Alcala, Chaleco, Chano Lobato, Sernita de Jerez

GUITARISTS: Ricardo Modrego, Rafael Nogales, Carlos Sanchez, Currito de Jerez

PROGRAM: "Eritana," "Cana," "Baile Por Mirabra," "Viva Navarra," "El Amor Brujo," "Estampa Flamenca," "Concierto Espanol," "El Martinete," "Suite Of Basque Dances," "Suite Of Sonatas," "La Taberna Del Toro," "The Three Cornered Hat," "Triana," "Zorongo Gitano," NY Premiere of "Fantasia Galaica."

Company Manager: Kurt Neumann
Press: Martin Feinstein, Michael Sweeley, Edward Parkinson
Stage Manager: Roger Johnson

° Closed Sunday, January 16, 1966.
(16 performances)

38

Antonio (LC)
in "The Three-Cornered Hat"
Above: Alicia Diaz

Antonio

"Fantasia Galaica"
Above: "La Taberna Del Toro"
Ballets De Madrid

"Three Leaps". Left Center: "Gypsy Dances"
Top: (L) "Wedding Dance in Ecser". (R) "Bottle Dance"
Hungarian National Ballet

NEW YORK CITY CENTER

Opened Wednesday, January 19, 1966.°
Columbia Artists Management in association with The New York City Center presents:

THE HUNGARIAN NATIONAL BALLET And Folk Ensemble

General Manager, Istvan Feher; Artistic Director, Miklos Rabai; Director of Chorus, Miklos Paszti; Director of Dancers, Zoltan Matyus; Conductor, Rezso Lantos; Leader of Gypsy Orchestra (Primas), Istvan Albert; Technical Director, Vince Horvath; Choreography, Miklos Rabai, Dezso Letai.

SOLOISTS

Edith Varnai	Tibor Erdelyi
Imre Farkas	Sandor Sajti
Erzsebet Varga	Irdiko Erczhegyi
Anna Czako	Laszlo Tarczi
Geza Leka	

PROGRAM: "Kallai Kettos," "Two Songs," "Dance of The Hussars," "The Bottle Dance," "The Gypsy Orchestra," "An Evening In The Spinning Room," "Hungarian Gypsy Dance," "Gypsy Music," "Dance of The Shepherds," "Three Leaps," "Songs For Chorus and Orchestra," "Wedding In Ecser."

° Closed Sunday, January 30, 1966. (15 performances) Returned for 15 additional performances Wednesday, March 2 through Sunday, March 13, 1966.

"Double Dance"
Above: "An Evening In The Spinning Room"

41

Opened Tuesday, February 1, 1966.°
S. Hurok presents:

THE RUMANIAN FOLK BALLET
(Ciocirlia)
with
FOLK ORCHESTRA

Petre Nastovici, Director; Victor Predescu, Conductor; Ballet Master, Gheorghe Popescu-Judet; Artistic Director, Hero Lupescu; Choreography, Tamara Cap, Ion Ilie, Gheorghe Popescu-Judet, Iacob Lascu, Gheorghe Ilie.

SOLOISTS

DANCERS: Magda Popescu, Elena Tircolea, Ion Ilie, Marin Alecu, Gheorghe Ilie, Vasile Paraschivescu

VOCALISTS: Maria Stoica, Simion Pop

INSTRUMENTALISTS: Tudor Pana, Violinist; Damian Luca, Pan Pipes; Tony Iordache, Ilie Alecu, Cymbalom; Remus Bistrita, Clarinet; Ion Serbon, Kobsa; Dumitru Zamfira, Shepherd's Flute and Long Pipe

PROGRAM

PART I: Dance From The Oltenia Region, Hora Staccato, Come Out Moon And Look On Dance From The Almajului Valley, My Lad From Grui, The Flower Of The Slopes, Geamparalele, Suite of Dances From The Codru Mountains, Song From The Neadow Hora From Gorj, Dialogue On Two Cymbaloms, Bruil, Doina, The River Olt, Sirba, The Girls of Capilna, The Calushari Dance.

PART II: Suite of Walachian Dances, Dianca, Who Has Made The Song, Dear To Me Is The Somesh Dance, Moldavian Dance, Sirba In The Cart, This Is My Love, Ciocirlia (The Skylark), The Somesh Wedding.

Company Manager: Oscar J. Berlin
Press: Martin Feinstein, Michael Sweeley, Edward Parkinson, Myra Armstrong
Stage Manager: Kay Kingwill

° Closed Sunday, February 6, 1966 after a limited engagement of 8 performances. Returned to Carnegie Hall for 2 performances on Saturday, April 9, 1966.

Rumanian Folk Ballet

Jon Cristofori, Michael Uthoff, Ian Horvath, John Jones
Top: (L) John Jones, Richard Gain. (R) on top: Jon Cristofori, John Jones, in front: Ian Horvath
Scenes from "Olympics"
Robert Joffrey Ballet

NEW YORK CITY CENTER

Opened Wednesday, March 30, 1966.°
The Foundation For American Dance in association with New York City Center presents:

ROBERT JOFFREY BALLET

Director, Robert Joffrey; Assistant Director and Choreographer, Gerald Arpino; Executive Director, Alexander Ewing; Musical Director, Maurice Peress; Guest Conductors, David Epstein, Teo Macero; Lighting, Thomas Skelton; Ballet Mistress, Rochelle Zide; Production Supervisor, Jack Harpman; Production Assistant, Larry Metzler; Costume Supervisor, Regina Quintana; Choreographers, Gerald Arpino, Fernand Nault, Norman Walker, Anna Sokolow; Music, Peter Ludwig Hertel, Paul Fetler, Charles Ives, Anton Webern, Antonio Vivaldi, Teo Macero; Sets and Costumes, William Pitkin, Ming Cho Lee, Lewis Brown.

COMPANY: Charthel Arthur, Lisa Bradley, Zelma Bustillo, Diana Cartier, Ivy Clear, Edwina Dingman, Christine Hennessy, Susan Magno, Noel Mason, Marjorie Mussman, Margo Sappington, Donna Silva, Trinette Singleton, Frank Bays, Rex Bickmore, Robert Blankshine, Dermot Burke, Jon Cristofori, Luis Fuente, Richard Gain, Ian Horvath, James Howell, John Jones, Nels Jorgensen, Dennis Nahat, George Ramos, Don Richard, Michael Uthoff.

REPERTOIRE: "Viva Vivaldi," "Sea Shadow," "Incubus," "Opus '65," "La Fille Mal Gardee," "Contrasts," "Ropes," "Pas des Deesses," "Gamelon," and World Premiere of "Olympics" (Choreography, Gerald Arpino; Music, Toshiro Mayuzumi; Set, Ming Cho Lee)

NOTE: Music for "Sea Shadow" was changed to an original score by Michael Colgrass.

Manager: Wayne Richardson
Press: Isadora Bennett
Stage Manager: John Fenn

° Closed Sunday, April 3, 1966 after a limited engagement of 7 performances.

Arnold Eagle Photos

"Ropes"

Kenn Duncan Photo
"Opus '65". Above: Richard Gain, Lisa Bradley in "Sea Shadow" performed to a new score by Michael Colgrass

Zelma Bustillo, Richard Gain, Susan Magno, Diana Cartier, Jon Cristofori, Nels Jorgensen
in "La Fille Mal Gardee"
Above: (L) George Ramos, Michael Uthoff, Trinette Singleton in "Contrasts"
(R) Ivy Clear, Nels Jorgensen, Noel Mason, Lisa Bradley in "Pas Des Deesses"
Robert Joffrey Ballet

Diana Cartier, Ivy Clear, Jon Cristofori, Zelma Bustillo
in "Viva Vivaldi!" Above: Gamelan". Top: Jon Cristofori,
Susan Magno, George Ramos, Luis Fuente, Zelma
Bustillo, Ian Horvath in "Viva Vivaldi!"

Diana Cartier (top), Lisa
Bradley (below) in "Incubus"

Robert Joffrey Ballet

MADISON SQUARE GARDEN

Opened Tuesday, June 15, 1965.✿
S. Hurok presents:

MOISEYEV DANCE COMPANY

Artistic Director and Choreographer, Igor Moiseyev; Musical Director-Conductor, Nikolai Nekrassov; Coordinator, Simon Semenoff; Concert Master, Samuel Marder.

REPERTOIRE: Exercises On A Russian Theme, Exercises On Ukrainian Theme, Polka, Pontozoo, Lyavonikha, Bulgarian Dances, Trepak, Georgia, Sunday, Partisans, Sanchakou, Zhok, Old City Quadrille, Gypsies, Two Boys In A Fight, Gopak, Dance of The Tartars From Kazan, Yurochka, Suite of Old Russian Dances, Polyanka, A Day On Board Ship, The Three Shepherds, Khorumi.

Company Managers: Edward A. Perper,
Maxim Gershunoff
Press: Martin Feinstein, Michael Sweeley
Stage Manager: Jay Kingwill

✿ Closed Sunday, June 27, 1965.
(14 performances)

Moiseyev Dance Company

Dame Alicia Markova
Director of Metropolitan Opera Ballet

METROPOLITAN OPERA BALLET

Dame Alicia Markova, Director; Choreographers, Thomas Andrew, Todd Bolender, William Burdick, Katherine Dunham, Flemming Flindt, Zachary Solov, Alicia Markova; Ballet Mistress, Audrey Keane.

PRINCIPAL DANCERS: Edith Jerell, Fern MacLarnon, Hans Meister.

SOLOISTS: Sally Brayley, Miriam Ehrenberg, Patricia Heyes, Naomi Marritt, Carolyn Martin, Nira Paaz, Ivan Allen, Howard Sayette.

CORPS DE BALLET: Suzanne Ames, Susana Aschieri, Nicolyn Emanuel, Sylvia Grinvald, Rhodie Jorgensen, Pauline Knitzer, Diana Levy, Jeanette Maroulis, Melanija Mihalic, Janet Morse, Sharon O'Connell, Nancy Sklenar, Lee Wilson, William Burdick, Craig Crosson, Lawrence Eddington, Hubert Farrington, Martin Friedman, Josef Gregory, Harry Jones, Donald Mahler, William Maloney, Jan Mickens, David Milnes, Anthony Santiago, Franklin Yezer.

LEWISOHN STADIUM

Wednesday, July 28, 1965.

PROGRAM: "Les Sylphides," "Pas de Quatre," "Excerpts From The Sleeping Beauty," "Polovetsian Dances from Prince Igor" (Restaged by Vitale Fokine).

METROPOLITAN OPERA

Sunday, March 27, 1966.

PROGRAM: American premiere of "Echoing Trumpets" (Choreography, Antony Tudor; Music, Bohuslav Martinu; Scenery and Costumes, Birger Bergling, Philip Rosenberg; Conductor, Ignace Strasfogel), world premiere of "Concerning Oracles" (Choreography, Antony Tudor; Music, Jacques Ibert; Scenery and Costumes, Peter Harvey; Conductor, Alain Lombard), American premiere and new production of "La Ventana" (Staged by Hans Brenna after original of Auguste Bournonville; Music, Hans Christian Lumbye; Reorchestration, Hershy Kay; Scenery and Costumes, Robert O'Hearn; Conductor, Ignace Strasfogel).

THE HOFSTRA UNIVERSITY PLAYHOUSE

Saturday and Sunday, April 2-3, 1966.

PROGRAM: "Les Sylphides" (Choreography, Michael Fokine; Restaged by Alicia Markova; Music, Chopin; Costumes, Rolf Gerard; Pianist, Irving Owen), "Concerning Oracles," "La Ventana."

Louis Mélançon Photos

Patricia Heyes, Hans Meister in "La Ventana"

Miriam Ehrenberg, Patricia Heyes, Naomi Marritte, Nira Paaz in "Pas de Quatre"
Above: Kathryn Horne, Hans Meister, also top with Carolyn Martin in "Les Sylphides"

51

Sally Brayley (top), Edith Jerell (below), Ivan Allen (floor) in "Echoing Of Trumpets". Above: Edith Jerell in "Echoing Of Trumpets". Top: Anna Araeno, Ivan Allen, Naomi Marritte in "La Ventana"

Edith Jerell, Josef Gregory in "Concerning Oracles" Above and Top: "Concerning Oracles"

Metropolitan Opera Ballet

THE REBEKAH HARKNESS FOUNDATION DANCE FESTIVAL
Delacorte Theater, Central Park, N. Y.
August 30 through September 4, 1965

Executive Producer, William Ritman; Associate Producer, Bernard Gersten; Lighting, Nicola Cernovich; Production Coordinator, Andrew Mihok; Festival Liaison, Donald Saddler; Press, Peter Gravina.

Monday and Tuesday, August 30-31, 1965.

PROGRAM:

I. American Indian Dancers from St. John's Indian School, Laveen, Arizona; Thomas Fennell, Director.
COMPANY: Apaches, Harding Casoose, Richard Dawson; Papagos, Mike Chiago, Rico Thomas; Pimas, Leonard Enos, Sterling Manuel
PERFORMING: Round Dance, Shield Dance, War Dance, Hoop Dance, Snake Dance, Horsetail Dance, Eagle Dance, Rope Dance, Feather Dance, Farewell Dance.

II. "Beauty and The Beast" (Choreography, John Cranko; Reconstructed by Brenda Bolton; Music, Maurice Ravel; Costumes, Jon Maclain) danced by Clover Roope (Beauty) and Christopher Lyall (Beast).

III. Norman Walker and Dance Company: Cora Cahan, Jane Kosminsky, Dennis Wayne, Tony Catanzaro, Jeff Phillips, Roger Briant, Joanne Bruggemann, Dale Best, Marsha Wolfson, Pamela Ladimer, Alice Gill
PERFORMING: "Baroque Concerto No. 1" (Choreography, Norman Walker; Music, Vivaldi), and NY Premiere of "Trionfo Di Afrodite" (Choreography, Norman Walker; Music, Carl Orff).

IV. Myra Kinch and Company: Sally Holroyd and Christopher Lyall performing "Giselle's Revenge" (After the manner of Charles Addams; Choreography, Myra Kinch; Music Arranged by Manuel Galea; Costumes, George Horn; Decor, John Christian).

Jack Mitchell Photo

**Myra Kinch, Christopher Lyall
in "Giselle's Revenge"**

**Norman Walker
Above: Cora Cahan**

Zachary Freyman Photo

First Chamber Dance Quartet
(Janice Groman, William Carter, Lois Bewley, Charles Bennett)
and above left and right

DELACORTE THEATER

Wednesday and Thursday, September 1-2, 1965.

PROGRAM:

I. The First Chamber Dance Quartet: Charles Bennett, Lois Bewley, William Carter, Janice Groman performing "Recollection Of An Age" (Choreography and Costumes, Charles Bennett; Music, Francois Adrien Boieldieu), "Nocturne" (Choreography, Charles Bennett, Janice Groman; Music, Chopin), "The Coveting" (Choreography and Costumes, Charles Bennett; Music, Ernest Bloch).

II. Nala Najan performing Dances of India: NY Premiere of "Asthana Vidushi Natyam" (Classic Dance of Mysore; Music specially recorded in India; Costume, Jon Maclain), "Kathak" (Classic Dance of North India), and NY Premiere of "Chhau" (Masked Dance of Seraikella; Music recorded by Court Musicians of H. H. the Maharaja of Seraikella; Masks recreated in the Chhau tradition by de Monplaisir; Costumes recreated in the Chhau tradition by Jon Maclain).

III. Alba/Reyes Spanish Dance Company: Maria Alba, Roberto Cartagena, Carmen Suarez, Manolo Rivera, Pastora De Ronda, Lilian Morales, Nino Garcia (pianist), Paco Ortiz (singer), Juan Sastre (guitarist). Choreography and Artistic Direction, Maria Alba, Ramon de los Reyes; Costumes, Encarnacion, Vargas, Barredo, Ballardo, Quintana, Candelas, Rodriguez; Stage Manager, Maxine Glorsky.

PERFORMING: "Pinturas Andaluzas," "Aires Primitivos," "El Cabrerillo," "El Tacon Y La Bata," "Un Recuerdo De Zaragoza," "Fiesta Flamenca."

Zachary Freyman Photos

Jack Mitchell Photo

Nala Najan

Maria Alba
Above: First Chamber Dance Quartet

55

DELACORTE THEATER

Friday and Saturday, September 3-4, 1965.

PROGRAM:

I. "Pas De Trois" (NY Premiere; Choreography, Ron Sequoio; Costumes, Mel Juan; Music, Ricardo Drigo) danced by Katharyn Horne, Ron Sequoio, James De Bolt.

II. Jean-Leon Destine and Dance Company: Pearl Reynold, Eddy Walrond, Shirley Spiceur, Noble Ewje, LeRoi Fentresse, Louines Louinis, Freda Turner, Renee Poussaint, Audrey Mason, Herblee (pennywhistle player), and drummers Alphonse Cimber, Edner Calvin, Jacques Succes, and Rene Calvin.

PERFORMING: "Village Festival," "Fantaisie Musicale," "Slave Dance," "Yoruba Bakas," "Afro Chant," "Plante Cafe," "Drums," "La Legende De L'Assotor."

III. Murray Louis and Company: Gladys Bailin, Phyllis Lamhut, Bill Frank, and Roger Rowell performing "Facets" (Choreography, Murray Louis; Score, A. Nikolais; Costumes, Frank Garcia), and "Suite For Divers Performers" (Choreography, Murray Louis; Music, Vivaldi; Costumes, Frank Garcia).

IV. "Pas De Deux from Daphnis and Chloe" (Choreography, George Skibine; Music, Ravel; Costumes, Jacques Dupont), danced by Lone Isaksen, and Helgi Tomasson.

DELACORTE THEATER

Friday and Saturday afternoons, September 3-4, 1965.

PROGRAM:

I. Alba/Reyes Spanish Dance Company repeating performances of "Pinturas Andaluzas," and "Fiesta Flamenca."

II. Clover Roope and Christopher Lyall repeating performance of "Beauty and The Beast."

Lone Isaksen, Helgi Tomasson
Above: Clover Roope, Christopher Lyall
in "Beauty and The Beast"

Murray Louis

56

Alba/Reyes Spanish Dance Company
Above: Murray Louis, Gladys Bailin
in "Facets"

Jack Mitchell Photos

Maria Alba, Ramon de los Reyes
Above: Jean-Léon Destiné

57

CENTRAL PARK'S DELACORTE
THEATER

Opened Wednesday, September 8, 1965.°
The New York Shakespeare Festival (Joseph
Papp, Producer) and the Foundation For
American Dance (Alexander C. Ewing,
President) present the New York Premiere
of the new:

ROBERT JOFFREY BALLET

Robert Joffrey, Director; Gerald Arpino, Assistant
Director; Maurice Peress, Musical Director;
Thomas Skelton, Lighting Design; Associate
Ballet Mistress, Rochelle Zide; Associate Ballet
Master, Nels Jorgensen

COMPANY: Charthel Arthur, Lisa Bradley,
Zelma Bustillo, Diana Cartier, Ivy Clear, Edwina
Dingman, Susan Magno, Noel Mason, Trinette
Singleton, Robert Blankshine, Robert Brassel,
Jon Cristofori, Luis Fuente, Richard Gain,
Ian Horvath, John Jones, Nels Jorgensen, Dennis
Nahat, George Ramos, Michael Uthoff, and Ann
Axtmann, Esther Jaenn, Yvonne McDowell,
Ximena Quintana, Margo Sappington, Arlene
Shuler, Donna Silva; Martha Vaala, Frank Bays,
Rex Bickmore, Dermot Burke, Raymond Bussey,
Jorge Fatauros, George Montalbano, Haynes
Owens, Don Richard

REPERTOIRE: World Premiere of "Charivari!"
(Choreography, Lotte Goslar; Music, Michael
Colgrass, Jack McKenzie, Edgard Varese; Cos-
tumes, Raoul Pene du Bois), New York Premiere
of "Incubus" (Choreography, Gerald Arpino;
Music, Anton Webern; Costumes, Lewis Brown),
U.S. Premiere of "Gamelan" (Choreography,
Robert Joffrey; Music, Lou Harrison; Costumes,
Willa Kim), New York Premiere of "Contrasts"
(Choreography, Norman Walker; Music, Paul
Fetler; Costumes, Khan and Ruud), World
Premiere of "Viva Vivaldi!" (Choreography,
Gerald Arpino; Music, Antonio Vivaldi), World
Premiere of "Opus '65" (Choreography, Anna
Sokolow; Music, Teo Macero), Prologue from
"Olympics" (Choreography, Gerald Arpino;
Music, Toshiro Mayuzumi; Set, Ming Cho Lee),
"Sea Shadow" (Choreography, Gerald Arpino;
Music, Ravel, but new score by Michael Col-
grass created for City Center performance; Set,
Ming Cho Lee), "Pas des Deesses" (Choreo-
graphy, Robert Joffrey; Music, John Field;
Costumes, Anver Bey Khan)

General Manager: Alexander C. Ewing
Company Manager: Jack Harpman
Press: Isadora Bennett
Stage Manager: John Fenn

° Closed Sunday, September 12, 1965 after
5 performances.

Arnold Eagle Photos

Lisa Bradley, Ian Horvath in "Incubus"
58 Above: Luis Fuente, Ian Horvath, John Jones, Richard Gain
in Prologue of "Olympics"

Trinette Singleton in "Viva Vivaldi!"
Above: (L) Richard Gain, Lisa Bradley in "Sea Shadow"
(R) Noel Mason, Nels Jorgensen in "Pas Des Deesses"
Robert Joffrey Ballet

Nels Jorgensen, Lisa Bradley, Richard Gain
in "Gamelan"
Above: (L & R) "Opus '65"
Robert Joffrey Ballet

"Charivari!" (also above)
Robert Joffrey Ballet

Jack Mitchell Photos

Martha Graham
in
"Acrobats Of God"

FIFTY-FOURTH STREET THEATRE

Opened Tuesday, November 2, 1965.°
The B. de Rothschild Foundation presents:

MARTHA GRAHAM
and Dance Company

Produced by Gertrude Macy; Conductor, Robert Irving; Assistant Conductor, Harry Fuchs; Lighting, Jean Rosenthal; Production Assistants, William H. Batchelder, Marion Kinsella; Costumes Supervised by Ursula Reed; Sets, Isamu Noguchi, Dani Karavan, Jean Rosenthal, Ming Cho Lee.

COMPANY: Bertram Ross, Helen McGehee, Robert Cohan, Yuriko, Mary Hinkson, Gene McDonald, Ethel Winter, Linda Hodes, David Wood, Matt Turney, Robert Powell, Clive Thompson, Takako Asakawa, Carol Fried, Peter Randazzo, Juliet Fisher, Noemi Lapzeson, William Louther, Dudley Williams, Phyllis Gutelius, Gus Solomons, Jr., Jeanne Nuchtern, Ross Parkes, Janet Aaron, Juanita Londono, Diane Gray, Toni Shimin, Marcia Lerner, Rozann Stephens

REPERTOIRE: "Acrobats of God," "Appalachian Spring" (revival), "Cave of The Heart" (revival), "Circe," "Clytemnestra," "Diversion of Angels," "Embattled Garden," "Legend of Judith," "Phaedra," "Primitive Mysteries" (revival), "Secular Games," "Seraphic Dialogue."

PREMIERES: Nov. 2, "The Witch Of Endor" (Music, William Schuman; Setting, Ming Cho Lee) with Miss Graham in title role. Nov. 3, "Part Real—Part Dream" for the company (Music, Mordecai Seter; Setting, Dani Karavan). Choreography for both by Miss Graham.

Manager: Gertrude Macy
Press: Isadora Bennett
Stage Manager: Anne Sullivan

° Closed November 20, 1965, after a limited engagement of 22 performances.

Martha Swope Photos

Martha Graham (R) in "Acrobats Of God", and above with Bertram Ross, Ethel Winter

63

Matt Turney, Robert Cohan, Ethel Winter in "Appalachian Spring"
Above: (L) Yuriko in "Primitive Mysteries". (R) Helen McGehee in "Cave Of The Heart"
Martha Graham Dance Company

"Circe"
bove: "Phaedra" with Martha Graham (R)

Martha Graham
in "Phaedra"

Yuriko, Clive Thompson, Martha Graham
in "Legend Of Judith"
Above: Martha Graham as Judith

Bertram Ross, Martha Graham
in "Clytemnestra"
with Clive Thompson and Richard Gain in background

Martha Swope Photos

Bertram Ross, Linda Hodes, Martha Graham
Above: Gene McDonald, Bertram Ross, Martha Graham
in "Clytemnestra"

Martha Graham Company
in "Part Real—Part Dream"
Above: Matt Turney, Mary Hinkson, Bertram Ross

Martha Graham, Bertram Ross
in
"The Witch Of Endor"

Bertram Ross, Martha Graham in "The Witch of Endor"
Above: (C) Martha Graham (back turned), Robert Cohan, Bertram Ross
in "The Witch Of Endor"

Maya Plisetskaya as Odette, Nicolai Fadeyechev as Prince Siegfried
in
"Swan Lake"
Bolshoi Ballet

METROPOLITAN OPERA HOUSE
Opened Tuesday, April 19, 1966.°
S. Hurok presents:

BOLSHOI BALLET

Director General, Mikhail Chulaki; Principal Choreographer, Yuri Grigorovich; Conductors, Gennady Rozhdestvensky, Alexander Kopylov, Kiril Tikhonov; Guest Conductor, Arthur Lief; Assistant Director, Mikhail Anastasiev; Ballet Coordinator, Alexander Tomsky; Manager, Mikhail Lakhman; Interpreter, Helen Gillespie.

SOLOISTS

Maya Plisetskaya, Ekaterina Maximova, Natalia Bessmertnova, Rimma Karelskaya, Nina Sorokina, Maya Samokhvalova, Nicolai Fadeyechev, Vladimir Vasiliev, Vladimir Tikhonov, Mikhail Lavrovsky, Vladimir Levashev, Yuri Vladimirov, Alla Boguslavskaya, Ida Vasilieva, Larisa Dmitrieva, Natalia Kasatkina, Faina Kuznetsova, Natalia Pozniakova, Natalia Ryzhenko, Natalia Taborko, Elena Kholina, Elmira Kosterina, Dmitri Begak, Stanislav Vlasov, Esfandiar Kashani, Alexander Lavreniuk, Vladimir Koshelev, Valery Lagunov, Nicolai Simachev, Anatoli Simachev, German Sitnikov

REPERTOIRE: Swan Lake, The Nutcracker, Don Quixote, Giselle, The Rite Of Spring, Chopiniana, Raymonda, Divertissements, Highlights Program.

Company Manager: Edward A. Perper
Press: Martin Feinstein, Michael Sweeley, Edward Parkinson, Myra Armstrong
Stage Managers: Alexander Tsarman, Anatoly Pavlinov, John L. Moorehead, Jay Kingwill

° Closed Sunday, May 8, 1966 (24 performances) with a Gala Program for the final performance to be presented on the stage of the Met before its move to Lincoln Center. Bolshoi Company returned to Madison Square Garden Tuesday, May 17, 1966 for 7 additional performances, closing Sunday, May 22, 1966.

Maya Plisetskaya, Nicolai Fadeyechev
in "Swan Lake",
also above with Vladimir Levashev (L)

Maya Plisetskaya as Odile, Nicolai Fadeyechev as Prince Siegfried
in
"Swan Lake"
Bolshoi Ballet

Scenes from "The Nutcracker"
Above: Vladimir Vasiliev, Ekaterina Maximova
Bolshoi Ballet

Scene from "The Nutcracker"
Above: (L) Maya Samokhvalova (Queen of the Dryads), and
(R) Ekaterina Maximova, Vladimir Vasiliev
in "Don Quixote"
Bolshoi Ballet

Maya Plisetskaya as Kitri in "Don Quixote"
Above: (L) Eruk Volodin, Maya Samokhvalova, and
(R) Vladimir Tikhonov as Basil in "Don Quixote"
Bolshoi Ballet

Yuri Vladimirov (also above), Nina Sorokina
in "The Rite Of Spring"

Bolshoi Ballet

Dance of the Elders in
"The Rite Of Spring"

Yuri Vladimirov in "The Rite Of Spring"
Above: Nina Sorokina in "Chopiniana"

Maya Plisetskaya
as Raymonda

Bolshoi Ballet

Ekaterina Maximova as Giselle
Above: Act II of "Giselle"

Vladimir Nikonov, Natalia Filippova
Above: Mikhail Lavrovsky, Natalia Bessmertnova

Scenes from "Giselle"
Bolshoi Ballet

Natalia Bessmertnova as Giselle
Above: Ekaterina Maximova, Vladimir Vasiliev
in "Walpurgis Night"
Top: Yuri Vladimirov, Nina Sorokina
in "Flames Of Paris"

Liudmilla Vlasova, Stanislav Vlasov
in "The Doves"
Above: Mikhail Lavrovsky, Natalia Bessmertnova
in "Diana and Acteon"

Bolshoi Ballet

Final performance at Metropolitan Opera House, May 8, 1966.

HONORED GUESTS: Muriel Bentley, Annabelle Lyon, Maria Karnilova, Ruth Ann Koesun, Janet Reed, Leon Danielian, John Kriza, Jerome Robbins, Alexandra Danilova, Eugenia Delarova, Martha Graham, Mia Slavenska, Muriel Stuart, Frederic Franklin, Jose Greco, Igor Youskevitch, Lucia Chase, Melissa Hayden, Alicia Markova, Ruth Page, Andre Eglevsky, Michael Kidd, Hugh Laing, Antony Tudor, Janet Collins, Agnes De Mille, Felia Doubrovska, Maria Gambarelli, Tamara Toumanova, Anton Dolin, Eugene Loring, Pierre Vladimiroff, Hilda Butsova, Carmen de Lavallade, Nathalie Krassovska, Neannette Lauret, Sono Osato, Aubrey Hitchins, Lupe Serrano, James Starbuck, Marina Svetlova, Marc Platt, Simon Semenoff, Zachary Solov

PROGRAM:

I. A personally guided tour to dancing at the Metropolitan Opera House conducted by John Martin, Dance Critic Emeritus of The New York Times.

II. "The Dying Swan" (Fokine/Saint-Saens) danced by Maya Plitsetskaya.

III. Act I of "Don Quixote" (Petipa, revised by Alexander Gorsky/Minkus) with Maya Plisetskaya as Kitri, Vladimir Tikhonov as Basil, Petr Khomutov as Don Quixote, Nicolai Kharitonov as Sancho Panza, Natalia Ryzhenko as Juanita, Ida Vasilieva as Piccilia, Erik Volodin as Gamash, Maya Samokhvalova as a Street Dancer, Nicolai Simachev as the Toreador, Vladimir Levashev as Lorenzo, Militsa Sukhinich as Lorenzo's Wife. Alexander Kopylov, Conductor.

IV. Pas de Deux from Act II of "Swan Lake" danced by Rimma Karelskaya and Nicolai Fadeyechev.

V. Acteon's Variation from "Esmeralda" danced by Mikhail Lavrovsky.

VI. "Flames Of Paris Pas De Deux" danced by Nina Sorokina and Yuri Vladimirov.

VII. Gopak from "Taras Bulba" danced by Vladimir Koshelev.

VIII. "Melody" danced by Natalia Bessmertnova and Alexander Lavreniuk.

IX. "Dunayevsky Waltz" danced by Liudmilla Vlasova and Stanislav Vlasov.

X. Finale from Act II of "The Nutcracker" danced by Ekaterina Maximova, Vladimir Vasiliev with Soloists and Corps de Ballet.

XI. Epilogue: Grand Promenade by Honored Guests and The Bolshoi Ballet.

Wayne Shilkret Photos

Honored guests and members of Bolshoi Ballet at closing performance at the Metropolitan Opera House

HUNTER COLLEGE SECOND DANCE SERIES
New York, N. Y.

HUNTER COLLEGE PLAYHOUSE

Sunday, September 19, 1965.
The Hunter College Concert Bureau presents:

ERICK HAWKINS AND DANCE COMPANY

Choreography, Erick Hawkins; Music Conductor, Arthur A. Bloom; Composer, Lucia Dlugoszewski; Lighting, Owen Ryan; Sets and Designs, Ralph Dorazio.

COMPANY: Erick Hawkins, Bernardine Madole, James Tyler, Kelly Holt, Ellen Marshall, Rod Rodgers

PROGRAM: "Early Floating," "Geography of Noon," Premiere of "Naked Leopard," and first New York performance of "Lords of Persia."

Daniel Kramer Photos

Erick Hawkins, also at top right

Erick Hawkins
Above: Lucia Dlugoszewski

Thursday and Friday, October 14-15, 1965.

PAUL TAYLOR DANCE COMPANY

Choreography, Paul Taylor; Music, C. Jackson, Haydn, John Herbert McDowell; Sets, Alex Katz; Lighting, Jennifer Tipton, Thomas Skelton.

COMPANY: Paul Taylor, Sharon Kinney, Dan Wagoner, Bettie de Jong, Elizabeth Walton, Daniel Williams, Molly Moore, Karen Brooke, Laura Dean, Twyla Tharp, Carolyn Adams

PROGRAM: "Party Mix," "Scudorama," "Duet," "From Sea To Shining Sea."

Paul Taylor
Above: "Party Mix"

"From Sea To Shining Sea"
Above: Elizabeth Walton, Dan Wagoner
in "Duet"

Betty de Jong and company in "Scudorama"
Left Center: Paul Taylor, Molly Moore in "From Sea To Shining Sea"
Top: (L) Paul Taylor, Molly Moore, Daniel Williams, Sharon Kinney in
"From Sea To Shining Sea"
(R) Paul Taylor, Bettie de Jong in "Scudorama"

Friday, October 29, 1965.

THE ROYAL WINNIPEG BALLET

Director, Arnold Spohr; Choreographer, Brian MacDonald; Musical Director, Carlos Rausch; Ballet Master, James Clouser; General Manager, J. Sergei Sawchyn; Stage Manager, Thomas Legg; Technical Director, Charles Renaud; Production Manager, John Graham; Presented by S. Hurok.

COMPANY: Sonia Taverner, Fredric Strobel, Richard Rutherford, Lynette Fry, Sheila Mackinnon, Bill Martin-Viscount, Beatrice Cordua, Wendy Barker, Beverley Barkley, Helen McKergow, Yemaiel Oved

CORPS DE BALLET: Brian Anderson, Sandra Begg, Richard Browne, Patrick Crommett, Stephanie Finch, Richard Foose, Donna Frances, Raymond Goulet, Hiller Huhn, Florence Kingsbury, Donna Kirkbride, Hans-Rudolf Knill, Dawn Macdonald, David Moroni, Shirley New

PROGRAM: "The Rehearsal," "Bitter Weird," "Aimez-Vous Bach?," "Pas d'Action."

Top: "Pas D'Action"
Below: (L to R) Arnold Spohr (Director), Sonia Taverner (Prima Ballerina),
Lynette Fry, Richard Rutherford

The
Alvin Ailey
American
Dance Theater

Alvin Ailey (lower front) and company

Friday and Saturday, December 17-18, 1965.

THE ALVIN AILEY DANCE THEATRE

Artistic Director, Alvin Ailey; Associate Director, James Truitte; Technical Director, Nicola Cernovitch; Production Assistant, Marilyn Bord; Choreography, Alvin Ailey, Talley Beatty; Decor and Costumes, Ves Harper.

COMPANY: Alvin Ailey, Loretta Abbott, Takako Asakawa, Miguel Godreau, Judith Jamison, Joan Peters, Lucinda Ransom, Kelvin Rotardier, Clive Thompson, James Truitte, Dudley Williams, Morton Winston

PROGRAM: "Congo Tango Palace," "Reflections In D," "Blues Suite," "The Road of The Phoebe Snow," "Revelations."

HUNTER COLLEGE PLAYHOUSE

Sunday, January 16, 1966.

LES FEUX FOLLETS
Canadian Folk Ensemble

Director, Michel Cartier; Choreography, Michel Cartier, Brian Macdonald, Gladys Forrester, Michel St. Louis.

SOLOISTS: Sam Serici, Marcel Chojnacki, Gavino Ramirez, Andre Denis, Pierre Thivierge, Maryse Raymond, Nicole Boyer, Sylvia Worth-Mason, Isai Zarate, Michel St. Louis, Andre St. Pierre

PROGRAM: "The Canadian Mosaic" in ten suites: The Plains, The West, Industrialization, Acadia, Neo-Canadians, The Pacific Coast, Nova Scotia, The North, The Laurentians, and Quebec.

(No pictures available)

Alvin Ailey Dance Theatre (also above)

Alvin Ailey

HUNTER COLLEGE PLAYHOUSE

Friday and Saturday, January 28-29, 1966.

THE NIKOLAIS DANCE COMPANY

The New Theatre of Motion with choreography by Alwin Nikolais presents "Galaxy," with solos by Bill Frank, Phyllis Lamhut, and Murray Louis.

Scenes from "Galaxy"

Above: Bill Frank, Gladys Bailin, Phyllis Lamhut, Murray Louis

"Galaxy" with Bill Frank, Phyllis Lamhut,
Murray Louis, Gladys Bailin

HUNTER COLLEGE PLAYHOUSE

Friday and Saturday, February 25-26, 1966.

ERICK HAWKINS
and
DANCE COMPANY

Choreography, Erick Hawkins; Composer, Lucia Dlugoszewski; Conductor, Arthur A. Bloom; Lighting, Owen Ryan; Designs and Sets, Ralph Dorazio; Costumes, Ruth Sobotka.

COMPANY: Erick Hawkins, Bernadine Madole, James Tyler, Kelly Holt, Ellen Marshall, Rod Rodgers, Barbara Roan, Penelope Shaw, Beverly Hirschfeld

PROGRAM: "Early Floating," Premiere of "Dazzle On A Knife's Edge," "Lords Of Persia," "Naked Leopard," New York premiere of "Cantilever."

Photos by D. Drinkwater, Daniel Kramer and John Geraci

Erick Hawkins in
"Geography Of Noon"

Erick Hawkins, also above in
"Early Floating"

Jack Mitchell Photo

Robert Powell, Glen Tetley, Linda Hodes
in
"Pierrot Lunaire"

HUNTER COLLEGE PLAYHOUSE

Friday and Saturday, April 1-2, 1966.

GLEN TETLEY AND COMPANY

Choreography, Glen Tetley; Music, Mordecai Seter, Arnold Schoenberg, Oedeon Partos; Sets and Costumes, Rouben Ter-Arutunian, Anthony Binstead; Lighting, Gilbert V. Hemsley, Jr.; Production Manager, Maxine Glorsky.

COMPANY: Glen Tetley, Carmen De Lavallade, Scott Douglas, Mary Hinkson, Phyllis Gutelius, Lynne Kothera, Micheline Wilkinson, Elizabeth Wullen, Wesley Fata, Ross Parkes, Phillip Rice, Gerald Schneider

PROGRAM: "Ricercare," "Pierrot Lunaire," "The Mythical Hunters" (U.S. Premiere).

"The Mythical Hunters"
Above: Scott Douglas, Mary Hinkson in "Ricercare"

94

Glen Tetley
in "Pierrot Lunaire"

Wesley Fata, Carmen deLavallade, Mary Hinkson
in
"The Mythical Hunters"

THERESA L. KAUFMANN CONCERT HALL SEASON
(92nd Street YM-YWHA, New York City)

Paul Weller Photo

Saturday, October 9, 1965.

HAL GREGO JAZZ BALLETS

Choreography, Hal Grego; Sets and Costumes, Harold Charles; Lighting, Dorothy Vislocky; Sound, Robert E. Fournier; Stage Manager, Gary Harris.

COMPANY: Hal Grego, Helene Nealon, Henry Riviere, Joetta Cherry, Carl Ayers, Barbara Munnis, Bob Normandy, Richard Mezatesta, Steven Kiewech, Jack Dano

PROGRAM: "Jazzplay" (Music, Ramsey Lewis), "Chicago '24" (Music, Elmer Bernstein), "Been So Long On Lonely Street" (Music, Elmer Bernstein), "Family Of Man" (Leonard Bernstein).

Saturday, October 16, 1965.

JOHN COY DANCE COMPANY

Director, John Coy; Costumes, Richard Palan; Lighting, Gary Harris.

COMPANY: John Coy, Graciela Atencio, Judy Dearing, Marcia Gaynor, Renate Guttwein, Maralia Reca, Raymond McLean

PROGRAM: "Prologue" (Music, Vitale, Bach), "Problem" (Music, McKenzie, Kraus), "Resolution" (Music, Poulenc).

Thursday, October 21, 1965.

BALASARASVATI

In a recital of Bharata Natyam, the classical dance of South India, with K. Ganesan (dancemaster), T. Ranganathan (miridangist), S. Narasimhulu and L. Sekhar (vocalists), and S. Dhanalakshmi (narrator).

PROGRAM: Alarippu, Jatiswaram, Sabdam, Varnam, Padam, Tillana.

Saturday, November 20, 1965.

MARIE MARCHOWSKY
SOLO DANCE CONCERT

Choreography, Marie Marchowsky; Lighting, Tom Skelton; Recreated by Jennifer Tipton; Stage Manager, Art Baumen; Presented by Mrs. Beatrice Dassin.

PROGRAM: "Prelude" (Sauter-Finnegan), "Ebb Tide" (Isaac Nemiroff), "After Toulouse-Lautrec" (Igor Stravinsky), "Age Of Unreason" from the "Goya Capriccios" (Alan Hovhaness, Bela Bartok), "Three Amiable Foibles, Opus I" (Paul Bowles), "Cantos Femeninos" (Carlos Surinac), "Rites De Passage" (Lukas Foss), and premiere of "Three Amiable Foibles, Opus II" (Paul Bowles).

H. Swahn Photo

Jean Erdman
Above: Marie Marchowsky

Sunday, November 28, 1965.

JEAN ERDMAN'S DANCE COMPANY

in

"THE COACH WITH SIX INSIDES"

Conceived, Written and Staged by Jean Erdman; Lighting Design, Carol Hoover; Slide Projection Design, Milton Howarth.

COMPANY: Jean Erdman, Anita Dangler, Gail Ryan, Michael Prince, Van Dexter

MUSICIANS: Teiji Ito, Genji Ito, Peter Berry

PROGRAM: In three acts: Act I—Time: Past Present (Harry Me) The Fall, Wake and Reappearance of A Certain Party. Act II—Time: Future Present (Marry Me) Chips Off The Old Block. Act III—Time: Future Past (Bury Me) His Gadabout in Her Day.

Sunday, December 5, 1965.

BENNINGTON COLLEGE DANCE GROUP

Directors, William Bales, Jack Moore, Martha Wittman; Musical Director, Josef Wittman; Design Supervision, William Sherman; Costume Coordinator, Poppy Lagodmos; Stage Managers, Natalie Orloff, Martha Armstrong, Gary Harris, Dennis Parichy.

GUEST ARTISTS: Martha Wittman, Jack Moore

COMPANY: Martha Armstrong, Wendy Moscow, Joanne Robinson, Linda Wilder, Reuben James Edinger, Wendy Summit, Kathleen Haynes, Catherine Stern, Harry Sheppard, Susanne Snyder, Marc Ozanich, Laurie Freedman, Susan Slovak, David Krohn, Ruth Bauer, Holly Barrett, Verna Rakofsky, Risa Jaroslow, Sharon Johanson, Janis Beaver, Leslie Berg, Jane Elkington, Daryl Hartshorne.

PROGRAM: "Straight Up And Down!" (Music, Eric Dolphy; Choreography, Susan Slovak), "Threshold" (Music, Arthur Honneger; Choreography, Wendy Summit), "In And Out Of The Game" (Music, Manos Hadjikdakis, Mikos Theodorakis; Choreography, Linda Wilder), "Swingshift" (Music, Ornette Coleman, Jimmy Guiffre, Thelonius Monk; Choreography, Susanne Snyder, Marc Ozanich), "Breathe On This Mirror" (Music, Igor Stravinsky; Choreography, Laurie Freedman), "Unkind Farewell" (Music, Mose Allison; Choreography, Ruth Bauer), "Hourglass" (Music, Malcolm Arnold; Choreography, Kathleen Haynes), "Night Pieces" (Music, Louis Calabro; Choreography, David Krohn), "Vintage Riff" (Music, Shaw, Herman, Moten & Hayes, Eubie Blake, Willemetz-Charles-Yvain; Choreography, Jack Moore).

Saturday, December 11, 1965.

BARD THEATRE OF DANCE AND DRAMA

Conceived, Directed and Choreographed by Ana Itelman; Set, Stuart Whyte; Lighting, Spencer Mosse; Sound Technician, Christian Komp; Production Managers, Lois Phillips, Richild Springer; Stage Managers, Jo Ann Shay, Gary Harris, Ray Beckett.

COMPANY: Ana Itelman, Collette Barry, Alice Wislocki, Elizabeth Karrick, Richild Springer, Judith Lipgar, Gail Grisetti, Jamie Norton, Marion Tarr, Diane Wyle, Alan Just, Susan Abelson, Carla Sayers, Emily Grieg, Marya Lebensohn, William Driver, Mark Gorbulew, Jeffrey Rochlis, Andrew Knapp

PROGRAM: "House Of Doors" (Based on "The House of Bernarda Alba;" Music, Carlos Surinach), Premiere of "Three Rivers" (Music, Joaquin Rodrigo), "There's A Dead Horse In The Bathtub And Other Perplexities."

J. Wittman Photo

Ana Itelman in
"There's A Dead Horse In The Bathtub And Other Perplexities"
Above: Jack Moore in "Vintage Riff"
Top: Jean Erdman in "The Coach With Six Insides" **97**

KAUFMANN CONCERT HALL

Saturday, December 18, 1965.

MANHATTAN FESTIVAL BALLET

COMPANY: Donna Baldwin, Linda Carole, Helyn Douglas, Durine Dieters, Mari DiLena, Jill Brooks, Christina Stojanoff, Bryna Marcus, Bjarne Buchtrup, James DeBolt, Steven Gross, Ron Sequoio, Robert Ossorio

PROGRAM: Premiere of "Il Ottocento" (Music, Domenico Cimarosa; Arranged by Arthur Benjamin; Choreography, Ron Sequoio; Decor, Costumes, Mel Juan), "Once Upon A Time" (Music, Alberto Ginastera; Songs, Orff; Choreography, Marvin Gordon; Decor, Robert Rappaport), Premiere of "Valse D'Ete" (Commissioned by Rebekah Harkness Foundation; Music, Alexander Glazounov; Choreography, Ron Sequoio; Costumes, Milo Morrow), "The Wind's Bride" (Music, Claude Debussy; Choreography, Ron Sequoio), "Bach To Bach" (Music, Johann Sebastian Bach; Sung and Swung by The Swingle Singers; Choreography, Ron Sequoio; Costumes, Helaine Clark; Decor, David Budd).

Saturday, January 8, 1966.

BERTRAM ROSS AND DANCE COMPANY

Choreography, Bertram Ross; Music, Walter Caldon and Eugene Lester; Costumes, Betty Carol, Susumu, Ursula Reed; Lighting, Karen Jacobson; Masks and Graphic Design, Noberto Chiesa; Stage Managers, Karen Jacobson, Gary Harris, Dennis Ward.

COMPANY: Bertram Ross, Matt Turney, Robert Powell, Noemi Lapzeson, Alex Giannini, Judith Hogan, Jeanne Nuchtern, Ross Parkes, Avner Vered

PROGRAM: "Triangle" (Caldon), "Holy Holy" (Lester), "Untitled" (Caldon).

Saturday, January 22, 1966.

BERTRAM ROSS AND DANCE COMPANY

PROGRAM: "If Only" (Tape recorded by Simon Nuchtern), "Holy Holy" (Eugene Lester), "Breakup" (Walter Caldon).

Sunday, January 23, 1966.

GLORIA CONTRERAS DANCE GROUP

Artistic Director and Choreographer, Gloria Contreras; Costumes, Stanze Peterson; Tapes, Jan Surjala; Stage Managers, Gary Harris, Dennis Ward.

COMPANY: Gloria Contreras, Kathleen Carlin, Amelia Fatt, Polly Harding, Claire Kropf, Carol Purcell, Wynne Schwartz, Lynne Taylor, Edward de Soto, Stanze Peterson, Ronald Watson

PROGRAM: Premiere of "Sonata" (Music, Igor Stravinsky), "Bhakti" (Formerly "Eioua;" Music, Guillaume de Machaut), "Allusions" (Music, Anton Webern).

Matt Turney, Bertram Ross in "Breakup"
Above: Robert Powell, Bertram Ross in "Breakup"
Top: Ron Sequoio Company

KAUFMANN CONCERT HALL

Saturday, January 29, 1966.

PAUL SANASARDO DANCE COMPANY

Choreography, Paul Sanasardo; Costumes; Abigail Ewert; Lighting, Nicola Cernovich; Sound Engineer, Jan Syrjala.

COMPANY: Paul Sanasardo, Diane Germaine, Manuel Alum, Elina Mooney, Willa Kahn, Cliff Keuter, Judith Blackstone, Sara Rudner, Barbara Dolgin, Loretta Abbott, Sally Bowden, Regina Axelrod, Strody Meekins, Mark Franko

PROGRAM: Premiere of "Fatal Birds" (Alberto Ginastera), Premiere of "An Earthly Distance" (Henry), Premiere of "The Animal's Eye" (Schoenberg), "Forward In The Dark" (Zoltan Kodaly), "Metallics" (Cowell/Badings).

Wednesday, February 2, 1966.

YURIKO AND DANCE COMPANY

Choreography and Costumes, Yuriko; Decor and Lighting, Gary Harris; Costumes Executed by Ursula Reed; Special Guest Conductor-Pianist, Alan Hovhaness; Pianist, Edward Muller; Voice, Terrance Hawkins; Stage Manager, Dennis Ward.

GUEST ARTISTS: Clive Thompson, Patricia Christopher

COMPANY: Yuriko, Diane Gray, Kyungja Huh, Takako Kawakami, Juanita Londono, Anna Price, Anne Marie Rychiger, Rozann Stephens

PROGRAM: "Three Dances" (Hovhaness), "Wanderers" (Hovhaness), Premiere of "Tragic Memory" (Jolivet), "Wind Drum" (Poem and Music by Hovhaness), "Forgotten One" (Hovhaness), "The Cry" (Jolivet), Premiere of "Celebrations" (Vivaldi).

Sunday, February 6, 1966.

ISRAELI FOLK DANCE

Choreography, Fred Berk; Lights, Gary Harris; Stage Manager, Dennis Ward.

HEBRAICA DANCERS: Francine Berman, Joanne Bernstein, Bruce Block, Alan Bloom, Susan Brody, Laurie Finck, Neil Golin, Jonathan Handler, Tilda Jarolim, Adinah Margolis, Mark Markofsky, Larry Marks, Phil Siller

YMHA FOLK DANCE GROUP: Marcia Adelson, Lynda Aussenberg, Janie Barnett, Zeeva Benathen, Gail Braun, Livia Drapkin, Shannon Gilden, Debbie Kops, Ruth Levinson, Suzi Reimer

PROGRAM: Shalom, In The Vineyards, Desert, Around The Campfire, Folkdance Medley, At A Marketplace, In A Fishing Village.

Wednesday, February 9, 1966.

KOISABURO NISHIKAWA AND COMPANY

in

"An Evening Of Classical Japanese Dance"

COMPANY: Koisaburo Nishikawa, Ukon Nishikawa, Koijiro Nishikawa

PROGRAM: Kakashi (The Scarecrow), Kotobuki Sambaso (Congratulatory Dance), Fujimusume (The Wisteria Maiden), Yado No Tsuki (Moon Over The Inn).

Yuriko

Above: Paul Sanasardo, Diane Germaine in "Fatal Birds"

99

KAUFMANN CONCERT HALL

Saturday, February 26, 1966.

PAUL SANASARDO DANCE COMPANY

Lighting, John Dodd; Sound Engineer, Jan Syrjala; Stage Managers, Gary Harris, Dennis Ward.

COMPANY: Diane Germaine, Manuel Alum, Elina Mooney, Willa Kahn, Cliff Keuter, Judith Blackstone, Sara Rudner, Barbara Dolgin, Sally Bowden, Strody Meekins, Mark Franko, Laura Dean

GUEST DANCER: Kenneth King

PROGRAM: "The Offering" (Choreography, Manuel Alum; Music, Krzysztof Penderecki), "Broken Voyage" (Choreography, Judith Blackstone; Music, Antonio Vivaldi), "Storm" (Choreography, Manuel Alum; Music, Juliusz Luciuk), "Recurring Dream" (Choreography, Diane Germaine; Music, Edgar Varese, Tod Dockstader; Costumes, Tod Gardner), "Breakthrough" (Choreography, Barbara Dolgin; Music, Stanley Walden; Costumes, Abigail Ewert), "Nightbloom" (Choreography, Manuel Alum; Music, K. Serocki).

Keith Brian Staulcup Photo

Right: Diane Germaine, Paul Sanasardo in "Metallics"

Kazuko Hirabayashi, Dick Kuch, Dick Gain (also right) Triad Company

100

KAUFMANN CONCERT HALL

Saturday, March 5, 1966.

TRIAD

Choreography, stage management, costuming and tape-sound equipment by the company.

COMPANY: Dick Gain, Kazuko Hirabayashi, Dick Kuch, Janet Aaron, Lynn Kothera, Carol Fried, Carla Maxwell, Jorge A. Shaik

PROGRAM: "To Know No Shadow," "The Romantic Fallacy," "Vignette For A Queen," "La Rondeau," "The Lodgers."

KAUFMANN CONCERT HALL

Sunday, March 13, 1966.

CHOREOCONCERTS
LAURA FOREMAN AND
COMPANY

Director, Laura Foreman; Manager, Evelyn Honig; Consultant, Isabelle Fisher; Costumes, James Waring, Thais Barry, Alice Schwebke, Remy Charlip, Abigail Ewert; Lighting, Gary Harris; Stage Manager, Dennis Ward.

COMPANY: Laura Foreman, Don Redlich, Gus Solomons, Jr., Marion Scott, James Waring, Judith Willis, John Wilson, with Lenore Latimer, Karen Kristen, Deborah Jowitt, Edward DeSoto, Edward Effron, Eric Hampton, Daniel Lewis, Laura Glenn, Carla Maxwell, Sara Rudner, Dace Udris.

PROGRAM: "Tambourine Dance" (Choreography, James Waring), Premiere of "Fast" (Music, Colgrass, Dissevelt, Bartlett; Choreography, Gus Solomons, Jr.), "Tangents" (Music, Brubeck; Choreography, John Wilson), "March" (Choreography, James Waring; Music, Mozart), Premiere of "Memorials" (Music, John Watts; Choreography, Laura Foreman), "From The Sea" (Music, Andre Jolivet; Choreography, Marion Scott), "Songs For Young Lovers" (Choreography, Judith Willis).

Saturday, March 26, 1966.

PAUL SANASARDO
DANCE COMPANY

Lighting, John Dodd; Sound, Deryk Waring; Costumes, Abigail Ewert, Elina Mooney; Stage Manager, Gary Harris.

COMPANY: Diane Germaine, Manuel Alum, Elina Mooney, Willa Kahn, Cliff Keuter, Judith Blackstone, Sara Rudner, Mark Franko, Sally Bowden, Strody Meekins, Laura Dean, Kenneth King

GUEST DANCERS: Eddie Effron, Abigail Ewert, Barbara Greer, Kyra Lober, Carla Maxwell, Clyde Morgan, Jo Ann Wiess

PROGRAM: "Interior" (Choreography, Elina Mooney; Music, Glanville-Hicks), "Now What, Love?" (Choreography, Cliff Keuter; Music, Lasry-Baschet, Moondog, Stravinsky), "Woodfall" (Choreography, Sally Bowden; Music, Free Form Improvisation Ensemble), "The White Shirt" (Choreography, Cliff Keuter; Music, Foss), "Quartet" (Choreography, Elina Mooney; Music, Lee Chernoff), "Crossplay" (Choreography, Cliff Keuter; Music, Pleskow), "Miniature" (Choreography, Elina Mooney; Music, Stravinsky; Clarinetist, Andrew Schenck), "Hold" (Choreography, Cliff Keuter; Music, Foss).

Saturday, April 2, 1966.

EDITH STEPHEN DANCE
THEATRE

Choreography and Costumes, Edith Stephen; Lighting, Gary Harris; Sets, William Anastasi.

COMPANY: Edith Stephen, Margaret Cicierska, John Coy, Cari Sandors, Maralia Reca

GUEST ARTIST: Alonso Castro

PROGRAM: "Inner Outer" (Shafer-Henry), "The Square Circle" (Traditional 66), "Stained and Other Windows" (Finke, Debussy, Moondog), "The Wrecked Tangle" (Joseph Dylewski), and Premiere of "The Forbidden Playground" (Morton Feldman).

Top Right: Manuel Alum, Sara Rudner, Paul Sanasardo, Diane Germaine, Cliff Keuter, Willa Kahn in "Fatal Birds"

Edith Stephen (also above) in "Inner-Outer"

KAUFMANN CONCERT HALL

Saturday, April 30, 1966.

PAUL SANASARDO DANCE COMPANY

Choreography, Paul Sanasardo; Costumes, Abigail Ewert; Lighting, John Dodd; Sound Engineer, Jan Syrjala; Stage Managers, Robert Brand, Dennis Ward.

COMPANY: Paul Sanasardo, Diane Germaine, Manuel Alum, Elina Mooney, Willa Kahn, Cliff Keuter, Judith Blackstone, Sally Bowden, Sara Rudner, Mark Franko, Strody Meekins, Laura Dean, Kenneth King
PROGRAM: "Two Movements For Strings" (Alberto Ginastera), "The Animal's Eye" (Arnold Schoenberg), Premiere of "Excursions" (Eugene Lester in collaboration with Jan Syrjala), "Fatal Birds" (Alberto Ginastera).

Thursday, May 5, 1966.

MIDI GARTH PROGRAM OF DANCES

Choreography, Midi Garth; Pianist, Howard Lebow; Lighting, Jennifer Tipton.

COMPANY: Midi Garth, Harriet Clifford, Karen Geiger, Florette Orleans
PROGRAM: "Voices," "Time and Memory," "Vivaldi," "Double Image" (Schoenberg), "This Day's Madness" (P. Schaefer, P. Henry), and Premieres of "Retrospect" (Anton Webern), "Summer" (Haydn), and an unaccompanied trio.

Thursday, May 12, 1966.

YASS HAKOSHIMA

In a program of Mime; Presented by The Japan Society.

PROGRAM: Geisha, Harakiri, Fisherman, Dictator, Puppet, Duel, Eagle, Dream, Ecdysis, Illusion, Slave, Labyrinth.

Elina Mooney, Cliff Keuter in
"The Animal's Eye"
Above: Manuel Alum, Judith Blackstone in
"An Earthly Distance"

Marion Scott
in "Psalm"

KAUFMANN CONCERT HALL

Saturday, May 14, 1966.

MARION SCOTT AND
DANCE COMPANY

Choreography, Marion Scott; Scenic Effects, Thomas Skelton; Costumes, Abigail Ewert, Remy Charlip, Malcolm McCormick; Lighting, Jennifer Tipton; Stage Manager, Gary Harris.

COMPANY: Marion Scott, Elina Mooney, Judith Blackstone, Sally Bowden, Barbara Greer, Lynda Gudde, Christine Kaufmann, Maja Lichtenfeld, Dimitra Sundeen, Margaret Williams, Joan Wohlstetter, Moss Cohen, Mark Franko
PROGRAM: "Psalm" (Jacob Druckman), "Going" (Henry Cowell), "Three Energies" (Luening-Ussachevsky), Premiere of "Breakpoint" (Carlo Gesualdo), "From The Sea" (Andre Jolivet), Premiere of "Jump! Jump!" (Gunther Schuller).

Saturday, May 21, 1966.

LUCAS HOVING
with
Nancy Lewis and Chase Robinson

Choreography, Lucas Hoving; Costumes, Lavina Nielsen; Lighting, Jennifer Tipton; Stage Manager, Gary Harris.

PROGRAM: "The Tenants" (George Riedel), "Has The Last Train Left?" (Henk Badings), "Variations On The Theme Of Electra" (Edgard Varese), "Icarus" (Shin-ichi Matsushita), "Satiana" (Erik Satie; Vivian Fine at piano). "Satiana" was commissioned by Connecticut College.

Monday, May 23, 1966.

RUTH CURRIER AND
DANCE COMPANY

Choreography, Ruth Currier; Costumes, Lavina Nielsen; Sets, Thomas DeGaetani; Lighting, Arthur Bauman; Stage Manager, Gary Harris.

COMPANY: Ruth Currier, Joan Miller, Jennifer Scanlon, Ann Vachon, Cliff Keuter, Daniel Lewis, Edward Effron
MUSICIANS: Violins, Dezso Vaghy, Dorothy Pixley, Setsuko Nagata; Viola, Tibor Vaghy; Cello, Leszek Zawistowski; Piano, Judith Olson
PROGRAM: "Toccanta" (Henry Cowell), "The Antagonists" (Igor Stravinsky), First New York Performance of "A Triangle Of Strangers" (Bela Bartok), Premiere of "Some Idols" (Francis Poulenc).

Jack Mitchell Photos

Midi Garth

Ruth Currier
Above: Lucas Hoving
Top: Lucas Hoving, Nancy Lewis, Chase Robinson

George Firmage, President
Jeff Duncan, Vice-President and Executive Director

MONDAYS AT 9
East 74th Street Theatre

Presented by Dance Theatre Workshop, Inc. (George J. Firmage, President; Jeff Duncan, Vice-President and Executive Director) Lighting, Owen Ryan.

Monday, November 1 and November 8, 1965.

PROGRAM:

1. "Songs and Processions" (Choreography, Valerie Bettis; Music, Theodore Newman; Design, Lonnie Dann) with Jane Laughlin, Carolyn Dyer, Mary Ehara, Carla de Sola, Margaret Beals, Clyde W. Morgan, Jeff Duncan, Ray Cook, Dallas Edmunds, Roger Morris.

2. "Road Signs" (Choreography, Deborah Jowitt; Incidental Percussion, Murray Ralph; Narrator, Margaret Beals) with Ray Cook, Carla de Sola, Carolyn Dyer, Mary Ehara, Lenore Latimer, Jane Laughlin, Clyde W. Morgan, Roger Morris, Rosalind Pierson.

3. "Dreams" (Choreography, Anna Sokolow; Music, Bach-Webern-Macero) with Ze'eva Cohen, Jack Moore, Chester Wolenski, Ray Cook, Jeff Duncan, Eddy Effon, Martha Clarke, Lenore Latimer, Peggy Cicierska, Laura Roth.

Valerie Bettis Co. in "Songs and Processions"
Above: Deborah Jowitt Co. in "Road Signs"

Jack Moore
in "Dreams"

M. Tarnay Photo

EAST 74th STREET THEATRE

Monday, November 15 and November 22, 1965.

PROGRAM:

1. "At The Hawk's Well" (Choreography, Mary Anthony; Music, Britten-Chavez; Costumes, Christine Loizeaux; Decor, George Deem) with Mary Anthony, Harriet Clifford, Brenda Dixon, Barbara Leeds, Ellen Robbins, Lois Lowenstein, Moss Cohen, Gus Rappange, Alex Giannini.

2. "Assays" (Choreography, Jack Moore; Music, Evelyn Lohoefer) with Selina Croll, Kathryn Posin, Linda Tolbert, Chester Wolenski, David Krohn, Clyde Morgan.

3. "Threnody" (Choreography, Mary Anthony; Music, Benjamin Britten; Setting and Costumes, William Sherman) with Mary Anthony, Barbara Leeds, Harriet Clifford, Moss Cohen, Alex Giannini, Gus Rappange, Ellen Robbins, Brenda Dixon, Lois Lowenstein.

Lida Moser Photo

Judy Latimer, Jeff Duncan in "Dreams"
Above: Linda Tolbert, Chester Wolenski in "Assay #5"

105

EAST 74th STREET THEATRE

Monday, November 29 and December 6, 1965.

PROGRAM:

1. "For A Fervent One" (Choreography, Ruth Currier; Music, Giovanni Pergolesi) danced by Ruth Currier.

2. "The Night Before Tomorrow" (Choreography, Ruth Currier; Music, Anton Webern) with Ruth Currier, Joan Miller, Ann Vachon, Judith Willis.

3. "Canticles" (Choreography, Jeff Duncan) Incidental Percussion by dancers Ray Cook, Jeff Duncan, Russell Falen, Deborah Jowitt, Kathryn Posin.

4. "Of Meetings and Partings" (Choreography, Ruth Currier; Music, Harold Shapero) with Ruth Currier, Daniel Lewis, Joan Miller, John Parks, Jennifer Scanlon, Ann Vachon, Judith Willis.

5 "Statement" (Choreography, Jeff Duncan; Music, Donald Lybbert; Decor, Barton L. Benes) with Ray Cook, Martha Clarke, Eric Hampton, Deborah Jowitt, Sean Nolan, Kathryn Posin.

EAST 74th STREET THEATRE

Monday, December 13 and December 20, 1965.

PROGRAM:

1. First New York performance of "Andante Amoroso and Adagietto" (Choreography, James Waring; Music, Gustav Mahler) with Gary Gross, Deborah Lee, Clyde Herlitz, Carol Marcy.

2. Premiere of "Dew Horse" (Choreography, Judith Dunn) danced by Judith Dunn.

3. "Journey To A Clear Place" (Choreography, Martha Wittman; Music, Pierre Henry, Pierre Schaeffer, Edgar Varese with sound effects) danced by Martha Wittman, Marc Ozanich.

4. "Poets Vaudeville" (Choreography, James Waring; Music and Musical Coordination, John Herbert McDowell; Words, Diane De Prima; Singer, Gretel Cummings; Lighting, John Dodd; Costumes, Remy Charlip; Banner and Hats, Charles Stanley) with James Waring, Marian Sarach, Deborah Lee, Carol Marcy, Edward Barton.

Ruth Currier Co. in "The Night Before Tomorrow".
Above: Jeff Duncan Co. in "Canticles"
Top: Ray Cook, Martha Clarke in "Statement"

**Ruth Currier in
"Meetings and Partings"**

EAST 74th STREET THEATER

Monday, December 27, 1965.

DANCES OF KOREA

DANCED BY: Sung-Hae-OH and Yungza-OH
PROGRAM: "Chan Dan Moo," "Soong Moo," "Boo Chae Choom," "Taell Choom," "Reo Shim," "Choon Hyang Chun," "Chang Koo Choom."

DANCES OF GHANA

DANCED BY: Seth Ladzekpo and Patience Kawkaw
PROGRAM: "Anlo War Dance, Suite I," "Akan Ceremonial Dance: Kete," "Anlo War Dance, Suite II."

EAST 74th STREET THEATER

Monday, January 3, 1966.

MARIANO PARRA BALLET ESPANOL

Choreographerrs, La Meri, La Quica, Juan Martinez, Carmencita Lopez, Mariano Parra; Staged and Directed by Mariano Parro; Costumes, Groen, Sisson, and Fernandez; Lighting, Owen Ryan.

COMPANY: Mariano Parra, Jerane Michel, Ines Parra, Mariana Parra, Dini Roman, Manolo Rivera, Leo Heredia (guitarist), Pepe Segundo (singer), Sandra Owens (pianist).
PROGRAM: "Evacacion," "Las Tres Mujeres," "Farruca," "Homenaje a Espana," "Fandangos de Huelva," "Soleares," "Playeras," "Valenciana," "Sacramonte," "La Mujer en Esperando," "Fiesta Flamenca."

Lida Moser Photos

Mariano Parra

Judy Dunn in "Dew Horse"
Above: Marc Ozanich, Martha Wittman in "Journey To A Clear Place"
Top: James Waring, Marian Sarach in "Poets Vaudeville" **107**

Saturday and Sunday, November 6-7, 1965.

MIMI GARRARD DANCE THEATRE

CHOREOGRAPHY: Mimi Garrard

COMPANY: Joy Boutilier, Susan Buirge, Sara Covalt, Rachel Fibich, Mimi Garrard, Lulu Goldin, Meikle Guy, Batya Hochman, Raymond Johnson, Donna Kerness, Wanda Pruska, Kaiya Schoonmaker, Jeanette Stoner, Janet Strader, Mary Ellen Thompson

PROGRAM: "Area," "Ash Sequel," "Mombi, Diggd, and Kiki Aru," "Family," "Flicker."

HENRY ST. SETTLEMENT PLAYHOUSE

Saturday and Sunday, January 15-16, 1966.

PHYLLIS LAMHUT DANCE CONCERT

CHOREOGRAPHY: Phyllis Lamhut

COMPANY: Phyllis Lamhut with Don Redlich, Sally Gross

PROGRAM: "Pastel," "Two," "Hands," and premieres of "Monody," "Incidentals," and "Voids."

Phyllis Lamhut
Above: Mimi Garrard Dance Theatre

Phyllis Lamhut

108

HENRY ST. SETTLEMENT PLAYHOUSE

Weekends from Friday, February 25 through Sunday, March 13, 1966.

MURRAY LOUIS DANCE COMPANY

Choreography, Murray Louis; Scores, Alwin Nikolais, Alwin Walker; Decor, Margo Hoff, Paul von Ringelhein, Murray Stern.

COMPANY: Murray Louis, Gladys Bailin, Bill Frank, Phyllis Lamhut, with Joy Boutilier, Susan Buirge, Caroline Carlson, Ann Carlton, Sara Covalt, Vicki Dils, Debby Gerson, Luly Goldin, Carol Hickey, Lynn Levine, Sheila Mason, Peggy Novey, Wanda Pruska, Roger Rowell, Mirali Sharon, Gloria Smith, Janet Strader

PROGRAM: Premiere of "Enigma," "Figures In Gray," "Interims," "Junk Dances," "Journal," "Transcendencies," Premiere of "Choros I," "Facets," "Landscapes" (revised).

Seymour Linden Photos

Murray Louis (also top right and center)

Jack Mitchell Photos

Phyllis Lamhut, Murray Louis in "Junk Dances"

109

HENRY ST. SETTLEMENT PLAYHOUSE

Weekends from Thursday, April 28 through Sunday, May 15, 1966.

ALWIN NIKOLAIS DANCE COMPANY

Choreography, Sound Score, Color and Lighting Designs, Alwin Nikolais; Costume Director, Frank Garcia.

COMPANY: Bill Frank, Phyllis Lamhut, Murray Louis, with Ray Broussard, Susan Buirge, Caroline Carlson, Luly Goldin, Raymond Johnson, Michael Podolski, Wanda Pruska, Roger Rowell.

PROGRAM: Premiere of full-length "Vaudeville Of The Elements."

NOTE: Company also toured U.S. during this season with a repertoire of "Allegory," "Sanctum," "Galaxy," "Bewitched," "Junk Dances," "Ante-chamber," "Trancendencies," "Reflections," and "Suite For Divers Performers."

Left: Alwin Nikolais

"Vaudeville Of The Elements"   Eric Sutherland Photo

"Vaudeville Of The Elements"

Faludi and Sutherland Photos

Scenes from "Sanctum" with Murray Louis,
Bill Frank, Phyllis Lamhut
Alwin Nikolais Dance Company

"Galaxy", also at top
Above: "Imago"

"Allegory"
Above: "Imago"

Berlin Photo

Alwin Nikolais Dance Company

JUDSON HALL

Thursday, March 24, 1966.

FRANCES ALENIKOFF'S THEATRE OF DANCE AND SONG*

Frances Alenikoff, Director, Choreographer, Dancer; Jerry Scott, Assistant Director, Dancer; Eva Marie Sage, Dancer; Bob Cohen, Singer, Accordionist, Guitarist; Program based on folklore traditions and choreographed in contemporary dance style; Costumes, Frances Alenikoff, Beatrice Corn.

PROGRAM: "Variations On Israeli Themes," "Songs, U.S.A.," "Welcome Sabbath Bride," "Songs From South Africa," "Shango," "Mazurka" (Choreography, Renate Aubert), "Fair Maid Is A Lily O." "Jig" (Choreography, Jerry Scott), "Polka" (Choreography, Renate Aubert), "Pavane," "Songs, Slavic and Macedonian," "Polyanka" (Choreography, Nikolai Petrov), "Israeli Suite: Morning In Galilee, Songs, Lamidbar and Debka," "Songs Of Courtship and Consequences," "The Tailor Dreams," "La Serena," "At The Wedding."

* Company toured U.S., Canada, and South America under the name of Aviv Theatre of Dance and Song.

Peter Yarrow Photo

Frances Alenikoff

Martin Freedman Photo

Carol Flemming, Mary-Ann Bruning, Jerry Scott in "Variations On An Israeli Theme"
Above: Jo LeChay Lion, Robert Fitzgerald, Frances Alenikoff in "Morning In Galilee"

EXPRESSION OF TWO ARTS THEATRE
New York, N. Y.

Performances December 4, 11, 18, 26, 1965.

COMPANY: Charles Weidman, Mikhail Santaro, David Hebel, Maya Doray, Carol Geneve, Amy Hebel, Patricia Norman, Nadia Yates, Louise Silver, Irene Dilks

PROGRAM: "Study" (Choreography, Charles Weidman; Music, Samuel Barber) danced by Charles Weidman, "Easter Oratorio" (Choreography, Charles Weidman; Music, Bach) danced by company, "From Bach's St. Matthew Passion" danced by Charles Weidman and David Hebel.

January 15, 22, 26, 1966.

PROGRAM: "Stumbling Into The Sea" by Mikhail Santaro, "In The Beginning" by Charles Weidman, "Impressions" by Charles Weidman, "Sea Questions" by Mikhail Santaro, Premier of "Fuerzas De La Noche" by David Hebel, "Le Gibet" with Charles Weidman, Mikhail Santaro, David Hebel.

February 2 through May 21, 1966.

PROGRAM: Charles Weidman's Impersonations of Ted Shawn, Ruth St. Denis, Martha Graham, Doris Humphrey, Ana Duncan, Mary Wigman, and Charles Weidman; "Dialogue Situation #2 (Choreography, Charles Weidman) with David Hebel, Carol Geneve, Irene Dilks, Maya Doray, Sue Salko.

MARVIN GORDON'S BALLET CONCEPTS

Founder, Artistic Director and Choreographer, Marvin Gordon.

COMPANY: Marvin Gordon, Jill Taft, Anita Agnese, Judy Joseph, Peter Hamperian, Jim Hovis.

REPERTOIRE: "Tapestry," "Spanish Courtesan," "Once Upon A Time," "Israeli Suite," "Lonely Man," "Movie Mementoes," "Jazz Satirica," "Triptych," "Metropolis," "Minstrels," "Parlor Game."

NOTE: New York based company toured U. S. during this season.

Marvin Gordon's Ballet Concepts (also above and right)
Top: Charles Weidman, David Hebel in
"Bach's Easter Oratorio"

Marjorie Tallchief

HARKNESS BALLET

George Skibine, Artistic Director; Donald Saddler, Assistant Artistic Director; Kresimir Sipusch, Musical Director; Regisseur, Felix Smith; General Manager, J. B. Cerrone; Conductor, Andrew Apostle; Technical Director, George Bardyguine.

BALLERINA: Marjorie Tallchief
PRINCIPALS: Lone Isaksen, Lawrence Rhodes, Brunilda Ruiz, Helgi Tomasson
SOLOISTS: Elisabeth Carroll, Panchita de Peri, Suzanne Hammons, Marlene Rizzo, Finis Jhung, Ali Pourfarrokh, Richard Wagner
CORPS DE BALLET: Salvatore Aiello, Kathleen Bannon, Bill Breedlove, Jacques Cesbron, Lili Cockerille, Roderick Drew, Avin Harum, Alexis Hoff, William Jacobs, Philip Kaesen, Miyoko Kato, Barbara Livshin, Bonnie Mathis, Carlyn Muchmore, Dale Muchmore, Vicente Nebrada, Karina Rieger, Robert Scevers, Donna Stanley, Sarah Thomas, Robert Vickrey, Georgina Vidal, Dennis Wayne, June Wilson, Richard Wolf
REPERTOIRE (1965-66 Season): "Sarabande" (Choreography, Skibine; Music, Couperin; Decor and Costumes, Jacques Dupont), "Feast Of Ashes" (Choreography, Alvin Ailey; Music, Carlos Surinach; Decor and Costume, Jack Venza), "Idylle" (Choreography, Skibine; Music, Francois Serrette; Costumes, Alwyne Camble), "Time Out Of Mind" (Choreography, Brian MacDonald; Music, Paul Creston; Decor and Costumes, Rouben Ter-Arutunian), "Highland Fair" (Choreography, Michael Smuin; Music, Malcolm Arnold; Decor, Costumes, Andre Delfau), "Ariadne" (Choreography, Alvin Ailey; Music, Andre Jolivet; Decor, Costumes, Ming Cho Lee, Theoni V. Aldredge), "Abyss" (Choreography, Stuart Hodes; Music, Marga Richter; Costumes, Andre Delfau), "Capers" (Choreography, Brian MacDonald; Music, Vittorio Rieti; Decor, Costumes, Peter Wexler), "Daphnis et Chloe" (Choreography, Skibine; Music, Maurice Ravel; Decor, Costumes, Jacques Dupont), and World Premieres of "Sebatian" (Choreography, John Butler; Music, Gian Carlo Menotti; Decor, Costumes, Jacques Noel), "Venta Quemada" (Choreography, George Skibine; Music, Carlos Surinach; Decor, Jose Capuletti), "Daughters Of The Garden" (Choreography, Donald McKayle; Music, Ernest Bloch; Costumes, Robert Thompson), "Macumba" (Choreography, Alvin Ailey; Music, Rebekah Harkness; Designer, Jose Capuletti), "Koshare" (Choreography, Donald Saddler; Music, Louis Ballard; Sets, Costumes, Robert Davison), "Fifth Piano Concerto" (Choreography, Robert Scevers; Music, Saint-Saens; Sets, Costumes, Lewis Greenleaf III, Harvey Hysell).

NOTE: This company was founded in 1964 and made its debut Feb. 19, 1965 in Cannes, France, followed by a lavishly praised international tour. Prior to its first US tour that began in October 1965, it inaugurated the new stage in the East Room of the White House. After completion of its tour of the States, it launched a second international tour of Europe, North Africa, and the Near East. Although headquarters are in Manhattan, it has not yet had its N. Y. premiere.

George Skibine   **Rebekah Harkness**

Marjorie Tallchief

Lawrence Rhodes, Brunilda Ruiz in
"Time Out Of Mind"
Above: Elizabeth Carroll, Panchita de Peri, Suzanne
Hammons, Lone Isaksen, Helgi Tomasson in
"Daphnis and Chloe"

Lawrence Rhodes in "Daphnis and Chloe"
Above: with Panchita de Peri, and top: scene from
"Daphnis and Chloe"

Harkness Ballet

Helgi Tomasson

Lone Isaksen (and above)
in "Abyss"

Serge Lido Photo

Brunilda Ruiz, Roderick Drew in "Sebastian"
Above: Marjorie Tallchief (on floor) in "Ariadne"

Helgi Tomasson

Harkness Ballet

Brunilda Ruiz, Ali Pourfarrokh in
"Feast Of Ashes"
Above: Rehearsal of "Ariadne"

Finis Jhung, Elizabeth Carroll

Harkness Ballet

Saturday, November 13, 1965.
Presented in association with The Brooklyn Ballet Association and The New York State Council On The Arts.

ALBA/REYES SPANISH DANCE COMPANY

Choreography and Artistic Direction, Maria Alba, Ramon De Los Reyes; Lighting, Nicola Cernovich; Technical Director, Maxine Glorsky; Stage Manager, Beverly Emmons.

COMPANY: Maria Alba, Ramon De Los Reyes, Roberto Cartagena, Carmen Suarez, Manola Rivera, Pastora De Ronda, Lilian Morales, Paco Ortiz, Juan Sastre

MUSICIANS: Pedro Cortez, Nino Garcia, Chinin de Triana

PROGRAM: "Sonatas Del Siglio 17," "De Canela Y Clavo," "Danza Del Molinero," "El Cabrerillo," "El Tacon Y La Bata," "Malaga La Bella," "Pescando En La Mar Serena," "Tanguillo De Cadiz," "Un Recuerdo De Zaragoza," "El Gitano," "De La Infancia Al Invierno," "Aires Primitivos," "Suite De Danzas Columbianas," "Fiesta Flamenca."

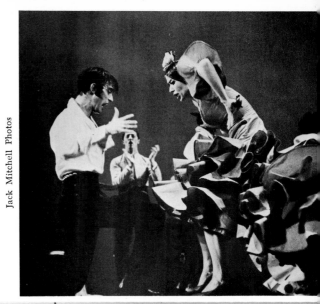

Jack Mitchell Photos

Ramon de los Reyes, Maria Alba (center) Spanish Dance Company
Above: Ramon de los Reyes, Maria Alba

Maria Alba

Jack Mitchell Photo

Jack Mitchell Photo

BROOKLYN ACADEMY
Tuesday, January 25, 1966.

LES GRANDS BALLETS CANADIENS

Founder and Artistic Director, Ludmilla Chiriaeff; Assistant Artistic Director, Fernand Nault; Artistic Adviser, Anton Dolin; Assistant Ballet Master and Resident Choreographer, Brydon Paige; General Manager, Uriel G. Luft; Conductor, Vladimir Jelinek; Lighting, Gilbert V. Hemsley, Jr.; Company Manager, Roger Rochon; Stage Manager, Paul Sullivan.

LEADING DANCERS: Irene Apinee, Bernard Hourseau, Armando Jorge, Veronique Landory, Christa Mertins, Vincent Warren

SOLOISTS: Richard De Vaux, Vanda Intini, Margery Lambert, Linda Stearns, Daniel Jackson, Erica Jayne

CORPS DE BALLET: Brenda Arevalo, Chantal Bellehumeur, Emily Byrne, Judith Karstens, Maria Lewis, Pamela Lynne, Judith Margolick, Shelley Osher, Jocelyne Renaud, Mairi-Helena Scott, Nicole Vachon, Leslie Andres, Myron Curtis, Rene Lejeune, William Thompson, Sanson Candelaria, Paul Wagner, Jill Courtney, Leslie-May Downs, Irene Diche, Mona Koelb, Patricia McDonald

PROGRAM: "Suite Canadienne" (Choreography, Ludmilla Chiriaeff; Music, Michel Perrault; Costumes, Mark Negin; Decor, Robert Prevost), "The Swan Of Tuonela" (Choreography, Anton Dolin; Music, J. Sibelius; Decor and Costumes, Silva Da Nunes), "Medea" (Choreography, Brydon Paige; Score, Georges Savaria; Decor and Costumes, Silva Da Nunes), "Firebird" (Revised Libretto and Choreography, Fernand Nault; Music, I. Stravinsky; Decor and Costumes, Robert Prevost).

Santos Photo

Margery Lambert, Armando Jorge
Above: Christa Mertins, Vincent Warren

Brydon Paige
Above: Brydon Paige, Margery Lambert

Armando Jorge, Christa Mertins

Saturday, February 12, 1966.

JOSE LIMON DANCE COMPANY

Choreography and Artistic Direction, Jose Limon; Costumes, Pauline Lawrence; Lighting, Thomas Skelton; Stage Manager, Jennifer Tipton.

SOLOISTS: Jose Limon, Betty Jones, Louis Falco, Sally Stackhouse

COMPANY: Jennifer Muller, Alice Condodina, Kelly Hogan, Lenore Latimer, Ann Vachon, Jennifer Scanlon, Laura Glenn, Carla Maxwell, Sarah Ford, Daniel Lewis, Fritz Ludin, John Parks, Peter Randazzo, Clyde Morgan, Avner Vered, Jim May

PROGRAM: "A Choreographic Offering" (Music, Bach), "Missa Brevis" (Music, Kodaly; Sets and Costumes, Ming Cho Lee).

Louis Falco

"Missa Brevis"
Above: Louis Falco, Sally Stackhouse in
"A Choreographic Offering"
Top: Jose Limon

Frederic Franklin (Center)
in
"Coppelia"
National Ballet

BROOKLYN ACADEMY
Saturday, March 5, 1966.

THE NATIONAL BALLET

Frederic Franklin, Director; Ballet Master, Oleg Tupine; Conductor, Ottavio De Rosa; Costumer, May Ishimoto; General Manager, Ralph Black; Stage Manager, Peter Turner.

COMPANY: Eugene Collins, Daniel Franck, Roni Mahler, Ivan Nagy, Andrea Vodehnal, and James Capp, Anita Dyche, Helen Heineman, Judith Helman, Lucy Maybury, Patricia Mideke, Julie Rigler, and Roger Bigelow, Karen Brown, Leslee Dean, Roberto Dimitrievitch, Drina Dimmick, Susan Gore, Harald Horn, Kathleen Laqueur, Michelle Lees, Michele Lynn, Jane Miller, Judith Reece, Kathleen Shipp, Patricia Sorrell, James Thompson, Betty Risen, Rafael Romero, Winthrop Corey, Edward Hanna, Oleg Vasilevitch, Caesar Tamburino.

PROGRAM: New York premiere of "Night Song" (Choreography, Francisco Moncion; Music, Harold Shapiro; Costumes, Ruth Sabodka; Decor, Lighting, David Hays), New York premiere of "Pas De Trois" (Choreography, Frederic Franklin; Music, Glinka; Costumes, Regina Quintana), "La Sonnambula" (Choreography, George Balanchine; Music, Vittorio Rieti after Bellini; Costumes, Patricia Zipprodt; Sets, Lighting, David Hays; Staged by John Taras), "Homage" (Choreography, Frederic Franklin; Music, Gounod; Costumes, Diane Butler).

Scene from "Homage", and above
"Les Sylphides"

BROOKLYN ACADEMY
Saturday and Sunday, March 26-27, 1966.

JOSE GRECO
And His Gypsies

Choreography, Jose Greco; Music, Composed or Arranged by Roger Machado and Jose Greco with interpolation by Albeniz; Managing Director, John F. Nonnenbacher; Company Manager, Oscar Abraham; Production Manager, Paul Haakon; Press, Warren Pincus.

COMPANY: Jose Greco, Nana Lorca, Antonio Montoya, Carol De Los Reyes, Rafael Garcia, Matilde Coral, Carmen and Justo Quintero, Barrilito, Josele, El Milionario, El Cancanilla, La Chichi. Guitarists: Manolo Baron, Beltran Espinosa, Paco De Lucia. Flamenco Singer, Pepe De La Isla

PROGRAM: "Andalusian Scene," "Divertissement," "Sevillanas Romanceras," "Fiesta Flamenca," "Idilio," "The Gypsy Camp."

Jose Greco (also above), Carol de los Reyes,
Antonio Montoya, Luis Heredia and company

Bruce Marks, Toni Lander
in
"Etudes"

Jack Mitchell Photo

BROOKLYN ACADEMY

Saturday, April 2, 1966.

AMERICAN BALLET THEATRE

Directors, Lucia Chase, Oliver Smith; Assistant to Directors, John Kriza; Regisseur, Dimitri Romanoff; Ballet Master, Enrique Martinez; Principal Conductor, Walter Hagen.

COMPANY: Lupe Serrano, Royes Fernandez, Toni Lander, Ruth Ann Koesun, Bruce Marks, Sallie Wilson, Eleanor D'Antuono, Gayle Young, and Susan Borree, Veronika Mlakar, Paul Sutherland, Janet Mitchell, Joseph Carow, Karen Krych, Ted Kivitt, Victoria Leigh, Edward Verso, Jeanne Armin, William Glassman, Judith Lerner, Eliot Feld, Ellen Everett, and Tom Adair, Diane Anthony, Amy Blaisdell, Karena Brock, Susan Casey, Camille Crosby, Cynthia Gregory, Virginia Griffee, Judi Griffler, Reese Haworth, Terry Hilton, Ray Morgan, Gilda Mullett, Alexandra Nadal, Paul Nickel, Terry Orr, Marcos Paredes, Christine Sarry, Gretchen Schumacher, Rosanna Seravalli, John Sowinski, Burton Taylor, Diana Weber, Richard Zelens

PROGRAM: "Interplay," "Grand Pas de Deux from Don Quixote," "The Wind In The Mountains," "Etudes."

Jack Mitchell, Fred Fehl Photos

"Etudes"
Above: Eliot Feld and corps in
"The Wind In The Mountains"

Ruth Ann Koesun
Above: "Etudes"

Richard Rutledge Photo

BROOKLYN ACADEMY

Saturday, April 23, 1966.

MERCE CUNNINGHAM AND DANCE COMPANY

Choreography, Merce Cunningham; Musical Director, John Cage; Decor and Costumes, Robert Rauschenberg; Lighting, Beverly Emmons.

COMPANY: Merce Cunningham, Carolyn Brown, Barbara Lloyd, Sandra Neels, Valda Setterfield, Albert Reid, Gus Solomons, Jr.

PROGRAM: "Suite For Five" (Music, John Cage), "Winterbranch" (Sounds, LaMonte Young), "Antic Meet" (Music, John Cage).

Marvin Silver Photo

Barbara Lloyd, Merce Cunningham in "Suite For Five"
Above: (L) Merce Cunningham in "Antic Meet"
(R) "Suite For Five"

Hans Malmberg Photo

Lida Moser Photo

BROOKLYN ACADEMY
Friday, April 29, 1966.

CONTEMPORARY AMERICAN DANCE

(A demonstration program for members of the Bolshoi Ballet)

PROGRAM:

I. Merce Cunningham Dance Company in "Suite For Five" (Choreography, Merce Cunningham; Music, John Cage; Costumes, Robert Rauschenberg) danced by Merce Cunningham, Carolyn Brown, Barbara Lloyd, Sandra Neels, Albert Reid

II. James Waring Dance Company in "Phrases" (Choreography, James Waring; Music, Erik Satie) danced by Valda Setterfield, Deborah Lee, David Gordon, Carol Macy

III. Anna Sokolow Dance Company in "Dreams" (Choreography, Anna Sokolow; Music, Bach, Webern, Macero) danced by Martha Clarke Ze'eva Cohen, Lenore Latimer, Kathy Posin, Laura Vachon, Ray Cook, Jeff Duncan, Eddie Effron, Jack Moore, Chester Wolenski

IV. Paul Taylor Dance Company in "Aureole" (Choreography, Paul Taylor; Music, Handel) danced by Paul Taylor, Bettie de Jong, Carolyn Adams, Dan Wagoner, Molly Moore.

Jack Mitchell Photo

Paul Taylor and company in "Aureole"
Above: Jack Moore (standing), Martha Clarke,
Chester Wolenski in "Dreams"

133

Ted Shawn
Founder-Director

JACOB'S PILLOW DANCE FESTIVAL
Lee, Massachusetts
June 24 through August 28, 1965
Thirty-third Year

Founder-Director, Ted Shawn; Associate Director, John Christian; Choreographer in Residence, Clover Roope; Press Representative, Lawrence Humphries.

June 24, 25, 26, 1965.

PROGRAM: "Zapateado" and "Garrotin" choreographed and danced by Jose Barrera, "Icarus" (Choreography, Lucas Hoving; Music, Shin-ichi Matsushita; Costumes, Lavinia Nielson) danced by Lucas Hoving, Chase Robinson, Patricia Christopher, US Premiere of "The Swan Of Tuonela" (Choreography, Anton Dolin; Music, Sibelius; Decor and Costumes, Eduardo Webster) danced by Christa Mertins and Vincent Warren, Guitar Solo by David Bernardo, "Farruca de la Alpargata" choreographed and danced by Jose Barrera, "Has The Last Train Left?" (Choreography, Lucas Hoving) danced by Lucas Hoving, Patricia Christopher, Chase Robinson, "Alegrias" choreographed and danced by Jose Barrera, "Grand Pas De Deux of the Sugar Plum Fairy and Her Cavalier from The Nutcracker" (Dolin after Petipa) danced by Christa Mertins, Vincent Warren.

Right: Christa Mertins

Philip A. Biscuti Photo

Jack Mitchell Photo

Lucas Hoving, Patricia Christopher, Chase Robinson

JACOB'S PILLOW

June 29 through July 3, 1965.

PROGRAM: "On The Hills By The Sea,"
"Solitude," "Golliwog's Cake Walk" danced
by Lisa Czobel, Alexander Von Swaine, World
Premiere of "Pushpanjati Shlokam" by Nala
Najan, "Los Disparates after Goya" (Music,
Metzl) danced by Lisa Czobel, Alexander
Von Swaine, "Dasara Pada" danced by Nala
Najan, "Epitaph" (Music, Bach) danced by
Lisa Czobel, Alexander Von Swaine, "Jati,"
"Sabha Vandana Shlokam," and "Alari"
danced by Nala Najan, "Marionettes" (Music,
Stravinsky) and Bavarian Country Dances by
Lisa Czobel and Alexander Von Swaine,
"Tosca" (Choreography, Dean Crane; Music,
Puccini; Costumes, Karen Mayer; Decor, Vla-
dimir Dokoudovsky) danced by Irene Apinee,
Dean Crane, Wish Mary Hunt, Daniel Siretta,
James Miller.

Right: Dean Crane in "Tosca"

John Lindquist Photo

Daniel Siretta, Irene Apinee in "Tosca"

JACOB'S PILLOW

July 6 through July 10, 1965.

PROGRAM: "Excerpts from Les Sylphides" (Choreography, Michael Fokine; Staged by Dame Alicia Markova; Music, Chopin) danced by Metropolitan Opera Ballet soloists Fern Mac-Larnon, Patricia Heyes, Carolyn Martin, Hans Meister, "Pas De Quatre" (Choreography, Anton Dolin; Music, Cesare Pugni; Staged by Dame Alicia Markova) danced by Patricia Heyes, Fern MacLarnon, Miriam Ehrenberg, Carolyn Martin, World Premiere of "Trionfo de Afrodite" (Choreography, Norman Walker; Music, Carl Orff) danced by guest artist Robert Powell and Norman Walker and his company: Jane Kosminsky, Dale Best, Marsha Wolfson, Pamela Ladimer, Alice Gill, Jo Ann Bruggemann, Tony Catanzaro, Jeff Phillips, Roger Briant, Cora Cohan.

John Lindquist Photos

Patricia Heyes, Miriam Ehrenberg, Carolyn Martin
Fern MacLarnon in "Pas De Quatre"
Metropolitan Opera Ballet

Robert Powell, Jane Kosminsky, Norman Walker,
Cora Cahan in "Trionfo de Afrodite"
Norman Walker Dance Company

137

July 13 through July 17, 1965.

THE NEDERLANDS DANS THEATER
(Dutch Ballet Theatre)

Artistic Directors: Hans van Manen, Benjamin Harkarvy.

SOLOISTS: Willy de la Bye, Milly Gramberg, Anne Hyde, Alexandra Radius, Marian Sarstadt, Charles Czarny, Han Ebbelaar, Jaap Flier, Gerard Lamaitre, Job Sanders, and Mabel Alter, Madeleine Felix, Kathy Gosschalk, Tiny van Pel, Sabine Vaessen, Mea Venema, Hans Hylton, Gale Law, Marten Molema, Joop Stokvis

PROGRAM: "Entrata" (Choreography, Job Sanders; Music, Otto Ketting; Decor and Costumes, John Law), "Pierrot Lunaire" (Choreography, Glen Tetley, Music, Arnold Schoenberg; Decor, Rouben Ter-Arutunian), "Septet" (Choreography, Benjamin Harkarvy; Music, Saint-Saens), "Opus 12" (Choreography, Hans van Manen; Music, Bartok; Decor and Costumes, Co Westerik, Jan van der Wal.)

JACOB'S PILLOW

July 20 through July 24, 1965.

THE NEDERLANDS DANS THEATER

PROGRAM: "Recital For Cellist and Eight Dancers" (Choreography, Benjamin Harkarvy; Music, Bach; Setting, Daniel Karman), "Symphony In Three Movements" (Choreography, Hans van Manen; Music, Stravinsky; Costumes, Nicolaas Wijnberg), "Omnibus" (Choreography, Hans van Manen; Music, Eddie Sauter, Jon Sibelius; Costumes, Nicolaas Wijnberg).

John Van Lund Photo

Nederlands Dans Theater in "Recital For Cellist and Eight Dancers"
Above: Jaap Flier, Kathy Gosschalk in "Pierrot Lunaire"

July 27 through July 31, 1965.

ALBA/REYES SPANISH DANCE COMPANY

Choreography and Artistic Direction, Maria Alba, Ramon de los Reyes.

PROGRAM: "Sonatas Del Siglo 17" (Scarlatti) danced by Roberto Cartagena, Carmen Suarez, Manolo Rivera, Lilian Morales, "De Camela Y Clavo" (Sequiriyas) danced by Maria Alba, Ramon de los Reyes, "Danza Del Molinero" (de Falla) danced by Roberto Cartagena, "El Cabrerillo" (Romo) danced by Ramon de los Reyes, Pastora de Ronda, Roberto Cartagena, Manolo Rivera, "El Tacon Y La Bata" (Tientos Clasicos) danced by Maria Alba, "Pinturas Andaluzas" danced by Roberto Cartagena, Carmen Suarez, Manolo Rivera, Pastora de Ronda, Lilian Morales, Ramon de los Reyes, Maria Alba and entire company, "Un Recuerdo De Zaragoza" (Jota la Delores) danced by Roberto Cartagena, Carmen Suarez, Manolo Rivera, Pastora de Ronda, Lilian Morales, "El Gitano" (Soleares) danced by Ramon de los Reyes, "De La Infancia Al Invierno" (Turina) danced by Maria Alba, Ramon de los Reyes, Roberto Cartagena, Pastora de Ronda, Manolo Rivera, Lilian Morales, Paco Ortiz, Juan Sastre, "Aires Primitivos" (Sastre) danced by Juan Sastre, "Suite De Danzas Colombianas" (Staged by Alonso Cano) danced by Roberto Cartagena, Pastora de Ronda, Manolo Rivera, Lilian Morales, Maria Alba, Ramon de los Reyes, "Fiesta Flamenca" (Farruca-Alegrias) danced by entire company.

John Lindquist Photo

Jack Mitchell Photo

Ramon de los Reyes, Maria Alba
(also above)

Maria Tallchief, Peter Van Dyk
in
"The Unfinished Symphony"

John Lindquist Photo

JACOB'S PILLOW

August 3 through August 7, 1965.

PROGRAM: "Kites" (Choreography, Al Huang; Music, Olivier Massaien; Costumes, William Sherman) danced by Al Huang, Pamela James, Suzanne Pierce, Santo Giglio, World Premiere of "Isle Of Loneliness" (Choreography, Myra Kinch; Music, Manuel Galea; Costumes, Jon Maclain; Decor, John Christian) danced by Myra Kinch, Christopher Lyall, Sally Holroyd, Peggy Florin, Phyllis Papa, "The Tent" (Costumes, Suzanne Pierce) choreographed and danced by Al Huang, "Cicada Song" choreographed, scored, costumed and danced by Al Huang, US Premiere of "The Unfinished Symphony" (Choreography, Peter Van Dyk; Music, Schubert; Costumes, Kalinowski) danced by Maria Tallchief, Peter Van Dyk, "Sleep's A Shell To Break And Spurn!" (Choreography, Al Huang; Music, Bruno Maderna; Costumes, Suzanne Pierce) danced by Al Huang, Suzanne Pierce, Pamela James, Santo Giglio, "Giselle's Revenge" (Choreography, Myra Kinch; Music, Adolphe Adam; Costumes, George Horn; Decor, John Christian) danced by Myra Kinch, Christopher Lyall, Sally Holroyd, Peggy Florin, Phyllis Papa.

John Lindquist Photo

John Van Lund Photo

John Lindquist Photo

Ralph Pierce Photos

Al Huang, Pamela James, Suzanne Pierce, Santo Giglio, also above in "Kites", and right in "Sleep's A Shell To Break And Spurn!"

Top: Myra Kinch, Christopher Lyall in "Giselle's Revenge"
Below: Al Huang in "Cicada Song"

141

James Howell Photo

Gerald Arpino, Alexander C. Ewing, Robert Joffrey

Lindquist

JACOB'S PILLOW

August 10 through August 14, 1965.

ROBERT JOFFREY BALLET

Director, Robert Joffrey; Assistant Director, Gerald Arpino; General Manager, Alexander C. Ewing; Company Manager, Jack Harpman; Lighting, Thomas Skelton; Associate Ballet Mistress, Rochelle Zide; Associate Ballet Master, Nels Jorgensen; Stage Manager, John Fenn.

COMPANY: Richard Gain, John Jones, Noel Mason, Dennis Nahat, Trinette Singleton, Zelma Bustillo, Diana Cartier, Ivy Clear, Edwina Dingman, Susan Magno, Robert Blankshine, Jon Cristofori, Ian Horvath, Lisa Bradley, Nels Jorgensen, George Ramos, Michael Uthoff, Charthel Arthur, Robert Brassel, James Howell, Marjorie Mussman

PROGRAM: US Premiere of "The Game Of Noah" (Choreography, Glen Tetley; Music, Stravinsky; Costumes, Scenery, Willa Kim), "Pas Des Deesses" (Choreography, Robert Joffrey; Music, John Field), US Premiere of "Incubus" (Choreography, Gerald Arpino; Music, Anton Webern; Costumes, Lou Brown), World Premiere of "Contrasts" (Choreography, Norman Walker; Music, Paul Fetler; Costumes, Khan and Ruud), "Sea Shadow" (Choreography, Gerald Arpino; Music, Ravel) danced by Lisa Bradley, Richard Gain.

Herbert Migdoll Photo

Jack Mitchell Photo

Trinette Singleton

Robert Blankshine

142   **Above: Richard Gain, Lisa Bradley in "Sea Shadow"**

"Contrasts", also center left and right. Top: (L) Lisa Bradley, Ivy Clear, Nels Jorgensen, Noel Mason in "Pas Des Deesses". (R) Diana Cartier, Nels Jorgensen, Zelma Bustillo, Richard Gain, Lisa Bradley in "Incubus"

JACOB'S PILLOW

August 17 through August 21, 1965.

PROGRAM: US Premiere of "Beaded Mask" (Choreography and Costumes, Pearl Primus; Music, Traditional) danced by Percival Borde, Edith Bascombe, Mary Waithe, "Chants" (Music, Traditional; Costumes, Pearl Primus) danced by Koko Ita, Mme. Nkoyo Ita, Mary Waithe, Edith Bascombe, "Earth Magician" (Choreography and Costumes, Pearl Primus; Music, Traditional) danced by Percival Borde, "Transcendencies" (Music, Alwin Nikolais; Costume, Frank Garcia; Lighting, Nicola Cernovich) choreographed and danced by Murray Louis, "Ashwadaka" (Music, Traditional; Costume, Pearl Primus) danced by Koko Ita, "War Dance" (Choreography and Costume, Pearl Primus; Music, Traditional) danced by Percival Borde, "Ntimi" (Costume and Music, Traditional) choreographed and danced by Mme. Nkoyo Ita, "Drum Talk" by Alphonse Cimber, "Impinyuza" (Choreography and Costume, Pearl Primus; Music, Traditional) danced by Percival Borde, "Kukulcan" (Choreography, Alonzo Rivera; Music, Jess Meeker; Costumes, Jon Maclain; Decor, John Christian) danced by Alonzo Rivera, Robert Thomas, Anthony Addison, Alfredo Moreno, Tom Leabhart, Thomas Quan, Thomas Naayen, Judy Congress, Eva Maxwell, April Beall, Sharry Dolvorich, Naomi Schreiber, Gaynor Cote, Naomi Rabinowitz, Janelle Thomas, Charlene Payton, Nancy Juhola, Ethel Sands, Elsie Johnson, Margo Barton, "Junk Dances" (Choreography, Murray Louis; Music, Arranged; Costumes, Frank Garcia; Lighting, Nicola Cernovich; Decor, Murray Stern) danced by Murray Louis, Phyllis Lamhut, Susan Buirge, Mimi Garrard, Sara Covalt, Janet Strader, Gladys Bailin, Bill Frank, Roger Howell, Louis Lamhut, John Redlick, Peggy Barcly, Ann Carlton, US Premiere of "Gbetu" (Music and Costume, Traditional) choreographed and danced by Percival Borde.

John Van Lund Photo

Murray Louis (center) and company in "Junk Dances"
Above: Alphonse Cimber. Top: Percival Borde

August 26 through August 28, 1965.

PROGRAM: "Indian Dances: Round Dance, Snake Dance, Shield Dance, War Dance, Hoop Dance" danced by American Indian Dancers Harding Casoose, Richard Dawson, Sterling Manuel, Michael Chiago, Leonard Enos, Rico Thomas, "Beauty And The Beast from The Mother Goose Suite" (Choreography, John Cranko; Reconstructed by Brenda Bolton; Music, Ravel; Costumes, Jon Maclain; Decor, John Christian) danced by Clover Roope, Christopher Lyall, "Peasant Pas De Deux from Giselle" (Choreography, Traditional; Music, Burgmuller) danced by Clover Roope, Christopher Lyall, "Indian Dances: Horsetail Dance, Feather Dance, Rope Dance, Farewell Dance" by Six American Indian Dancers, US Premiere of "Le Farceur" (Choreography, Clover Roope; Music, Ibert; Costumes, Doritt Dekk) danced by guest artist Christopher Lyall, and Charlotte Ames, Helene Themans, Leslie Smith, Denise Warner, Barbara Trevor, Fred Sumner, Sally Burton, Peggy McKane, Caroline Hubert, Ginger Sebert, Jimmy Lee Bickford, Max Philpot, James Murphy, Luis Villanueva.

Leslie Smith, Christopher Lyall in "Le Farceur"
Above: (L) Alonzo Rivera (center) and top right

John Van Lund Photos

AMERICAN DANCE FESTIVAL
Connecticut College
New London, Connecticut
July 24 through August 15, 1965

Charles Shain, Chairman; Musical Directors, Vivian Fine, Eugene Lester; Technical Directors, Sidney Bennett, Lawrence D. Berger; Publicity and Theatre Manager, A. J. Pischl; Stage Managers, Beverly Emmons, William E. Woolverton.

Saturday, July 24, 1965.

PROGRAM: Daniel Nagrin performing "Path; A Gratitude" (Traditional), "In The Dusk" (Ives), "Not Me, But Him" (C. Taylor), and "Indeterminate Figure" (Starer).

Bertram Ross and Dance Company: Matt Turney, Ross Parkes, Robert Powell, Alex Giannini, Noemi Lapzeson, Jeanne Nuchtern performing "If Only" and "Untitled" (Caldon).

Peter Basch Photo

Jack Mitchell Photo

Martha Swope Photos

Bertram Ross
Above: Daniel Nagrin

Matt Turney

Robert Powell
Above: Daniel Nagrin

AMERICAN DANCE FESTIVAL
Saturday, July 31, 1965.

PROGRAM: Ruth Currier and Dance Company with Jeff Duncan, and Joan Miller, Jennifer Scanlon, Ann Vachon, Judith Willis, Ronald Johnston performing "A Triangle Of Strangers" (Bartok), and "Of Meetings and Partings" (Shapiro).

Erick Hawkins and Dance Company with Composer Lucia Dlugoszewski performing "Cantilever," "Geography Of Noon," and Premiere of "Lords Of Persia."

Radford Bascome Photo

Ruth Currier

Erick Hawkins
(also above)

AMERICAN DANCE FESTIVAL
Saturday, August 7, 1965.

PROGRAM: Lucas Hoving with Patricia Christopher and Chase Robinson performing "Icarus" (Matsushita), Premiere of "The Tenants" (Riedel), and Premiere of "Satiana" (Satie). Paul Draper in selected dances from his repertoire, and a Premiere of a group work "Il Combattimento di Tancredi e Clorinda" (Monteverdi).

AMERICAN DANCE FESTIVAL
Friday, August 13, 1965.

PROGRAM: Yuriko and Company with Clive Thompson, and Takako Asakawa, Diane Gray, Phyllis Gutelius, Kywngja Ho, Anna Price, Rozann Stephens, Konomi Tsukasa performing "Three Dances . . . and the Wind," "Forgotten One," "Wanderers," "Wind Drum" (all with music by Alan Hovhannes).

Philip A. Biscuti Photo

Patricia Christopher, Lucas Hoving, Chase Robinson
in "Satiana"
Above: Chase Robinson, Patricia Christopher, Lucas Hoving

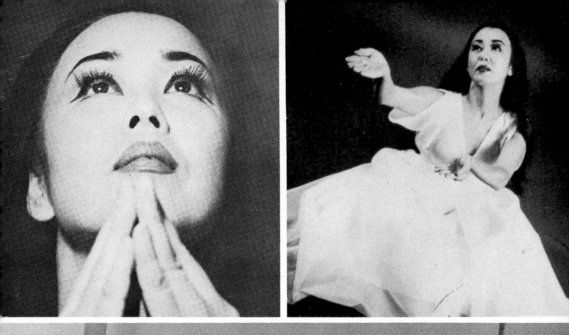

Daniel Nagrin, Libby Nye in
"Il Combattimento Di Tancredi E Clorinda"
Above: Yuriko

Philip A. Biscuti Photo

Jose Limon and Louis Falco
in premiere of
"My Son, My Enemy"

Martha Swope Photo

Saturday, August 14, 1965.

PROGRAM: Jose Limon and Company: Betty Jones, Sally Stackhouse, Louis Falco, Jennifer Muller, Alice Condodina, Ann Vachon, Lenore Latimer, Daniel Lewis, Jennifer Scanlon, Kelly Hogan, Laura Glenn, Fritz Krohn, Sarah Ford, Tamara Woshakiwsky, Carla Maxwell, Avner Vered, David Earle performing "A Choreographic Offering" (Bach), Premiere of "My Son, My Enemy" (V. Fine), "Missa Brevis" (Kodaly).

Jose Limon

Louis Falco
Above: Jose Limon

Jack Mitchell Photo

Jack Mitchell Photos

AMERICAN DANCE FESTIVAL
Sunday afternoon, August 15, 1965.

PROGRAM: Paul Taylor Dance Company: Elizabeth Walton, Dan Wagoner, Bettie de Jong, Sharon Kinney, Daniel Williams, Molly Moore, Karen Brooks performing "Junction" (Bach), "Duet" (Haydn), "Three Epitaphs" (American Folk), "Aureole" (Handel), "Scudorama" (C. Jackson).

AMERICAN DANCE FESTIVAL
Sunday evening, August 15, 1965.

PROGRAM: Repeat of new works: Lucas Hoving's "Satiana," and "The Tenants," Jose Limon's "My Son, My Enemy," and Paul Draper's "Il Combattimento di Tancredi e Clorinda."

Dan Wagoner, Bettie de Jong, Sharon Kinney,
Paul Taylor, Elizabeth Walton, Molly Moore in "Junction"
Above: (L) "Three Epitaphs". (R) Paul Taylor, Bettie de Jong

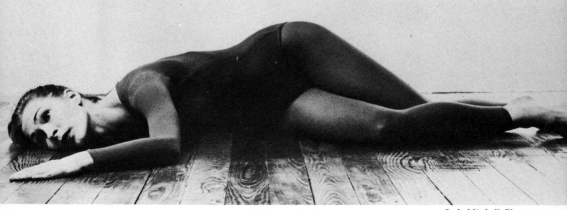

Jack Mitchell Photo

Bettie de Jong, Paul Taylor
in
"Scudorama"

Andre Eglevsky

THE ANDRE EGLEVSKY BALLET COMPANY
Massapequa, New York

Artistic Director, Andre Eglevsky; Pianist, Sonia Stein; Costumes, Dosi Sorokin; Stage Manager, Cyprienne Whelan.

GUEST ARTISTS: Maria Tallchief, Frank Ohman, Ramon Segarra, Melissa Hayden, Conrad Ludlow

COMPANY: Alba Calzada, Marina Eglevsky, Joanne Kutscera, Leslie Peck, Leslie Taylor, Susan Whelan, Jon Purinton, Christine Varjan, Trudy Snyder, Bevin Gilmore, Bojan Spassoff

REPERTOIRE (1965-66 Season): "Pas De Quatre," "Pas De Deux from Swan Lake," "Valse Fantasie," "The Nutcracker," "Ballinade," "Corsaire Pas De Deux," "Raymonda," "Pas De Deux from Stars and Stripes."

Maurice Seymour Photo

Marina Eglevsky, Ramon Segarra
in
"Corsair"

ANN ARBOR CIVIC BALLET
Ann Arbor, Michigan

Sylvia Hamer, Co-Founder and Artistic Director; Choreographers, Sylvia Hamer, Nathalie Branitzka, Marjorie Hassard, Pamela Magoon Rutledge, Nancy Carroll Abbey.

FEATURE DANCERS AND SOLOISTS: Nancy Abbey, Pamela Rutledge, Steve Stephenson, Homer Sprague, Linda Stamnitz, Margaret Ann Kulenkamp, Gay Shirey, Susan Woods, Cynthia Severance, Eila Bafs, Evelyn Falatane, Doris Smith, Rebeccah Oberkauff

REPERTOIRE: "Mendelssohn Concerto #2 in D Minor," "The Nutcracker Suite," "Swan Lake," "Giselle," "Coppelia," "Excerpts from Faust Ballet," "A Ballet of Divertissements," "Mozartiana," "Slumber Party," "Kinderszenan," "Concertstuck," "Mrs. Santa's Party," "Jewels," "Pastorale," "La Gambade."

**Linda Stamnitz, Nancy Abbey, Margaret Ann Kulenkamp, Gay Shirey,
Susan Woods, Cynthia Severance, Eila Bafs, Pamela Rutledge
Above: Sylvia Hamer**

ATLANTA CIVIC BALLET
Atlanta, Georgia
Thirty-seventh Season

Dorothy Alexander, Founder and Adviser; Robert Barnett, Artistic Director; Merrilee Smith, Co-Director; Associate Directors, Virginia Rich Barnett, Carl Ratcliff; Conductor and Musical Adviser, Robert Mann; Musical Director, Charles Magnan; Scenic Designer and Stage Manager, Charles N. Walker; Choreography, Costumes, and Decor, Robert Barnett, Carl Ratcliff.

PRINCIPAL DANCERS: Virginia Rich Barnett, Diane Gibson Bennett, Robert Barnett, Carl Ratcliff

SOLOISTS AND CORPS DE BALLET: Paula Burnette, Wimberly Cagle, Diane Clam, Linda Cook, Ann Goodrum, Callie Herzog, April Hopkins, Wendy Johnston, Jane Kapplin, Joyce Karlick, Hallie Kimmel, Ann Lardon, Paula Leveto, Christine Lyle, Kathy McGowan, Mary Jo Neal, Cheryl Pulver, Claudia Simmons, Ann Vorus, Peggy Williams, Missy Yancey, Dwight Arno

REPERTOIRE (1965-66 Season): "Fanfare," "Quatre Vignettes," "Llanto De Pueblo," "Grand Pas De Deux from The Nutcracker," "Danzon Cubano," "Suite Brilliante."

NOTE: On Tuesday, August 24, 1965, this company presented the first full-length "Swan Lake" ever produced in the United States; Staged by David Blair, who also danced Prince Siegfried with Lupe Serrano as the Swan Queen, Pittman Corry as Rothbart, and Dorothy Alexander as the Queen Mother. Kenneth Schermerhorn was musical director; Sets by Richard Gullicksen. Mr. Blair was assisted by his wife Maryon Lane.

Gaspar-Ware Photos

Barbara Hancock, Robert Barnett
in "Valse Pas De Deux"
Above: "Swan Lake"

Sara Ann Whiteside, Robert Barnett, Barbara Hancock
in "Pas De Trois"

De Casseres Photos

Photo Associates

"Dreams". Above: (C) Dwight Arno, Wimberly Cagle
in "Fanfare". Top: Sharon Bray, Kenneth Johnson,
Sara Ann Whiteside in "Pas De Trois"

Carl Ratcliff, Virginia Rich Barnett in
"Mountain Ballad", also top in
"Llanto De Pueblo"

Atlanta Civic Ballet

ra Ann Whiteside, Pamela Parker, Barbara Hancock in
"Valse". Above: Ed Cunningham in "Swan Lake"
Top: Madeline Upshaw, Dwight Arno, Polly Willis
in "The Nutcracker"

Carl Ratcliff, Virginia Rich Barnett
in "Gothic Ode"

Atlanta Civic Ballet

AUGUSTA CIVIC BALLET COMPANY
Augusta, Georgia

Ronald Colton, Director and Choreographer; Sallie Carlson, Associate Director; Connie Maxwell, Director of Wardrobe; Press, Suzanne Beaufort; Arthur Asbell, Carl Crosby, Guest Artists and Choreographers; Ballet Mistress, Zanne Beaufort; Lighting, Jack Hunt, Donna McCready.

COMPANY: Zanne Beaufort, Bonnifer Beaufort, Merry Dicks, Joanne McKenney, Nell Mobley, Julie Mulherin, Betty Darden, Janice Pellarin, Kip Price, Neville Riley, Harriet Schulman, Karen Carrington, Susan Presley, Kathy Stewart

REPERTOIRE: "Sleeping Beauty Waltz," "Poems," "Ballet Suite from Swan Lake," "Dans Le Bois," "Concertante Classique," "Pageant," "Trio," "Miranda and The Christmas Dream," "Recipe For A Ballet."

Frank Kinard Photo

Al Day, David McKinney, Ron Colton Photos

Nell Mobley, Zanne Beaufort, Bonnifer Beaufort in "Pageant". Above: Bonnifer Beaufort, Nell Mobley, Julie Mulherin in "Trio"

Arthur Asbell, Neville Ripley, Bonnifer Beaufort, Betty Darden in "Dans Le Bois". Above: Betty Darden, Arthur Asbell. Top: Ron Colton, Zanne Beaufort in "Pageant"

BALLET CELESTE
San Francisco, California

Directoress, Merriem Lanova; Executive Director and Business Manager, William Graves; Designs, Edo Pratini; Costumes, Ballet Celeste Associates, Lilli and Rex Rogers; Publicity, Frances Harris Allison.

SOLOISTS: Josefa Villanueva, Benjamin Reyes, Tomas del Solar, Donald Rodoni, Joyal Rodrigues, Merry Avery, Ramon Galindo, Kimberly Graves, Monica Prendergast, Robert DuMee, Teresa Bell, Alan Peters, Ludmilla Bogart, Lyn Jimenez, Carolyn Houser, Svenkarl Norrlander, Laurie Askinazy, Susan Owsley, Regina Ruggiero, Maureen Diangson, Benjamin Villanueva, Patience Valentine, Manuela Galindo, Sharon Thompson, Valerie Bussey, Regan Jessett, Gina Ness, Marilyn Trounson

REPERTOIRE: "Swan Lake," "Coppelia," "Bluebird," "Sleeping Beauty," "The Nutcracker," "Scheherazade," "Verdiana," "Goldilocks and The Three B's," "Chinese Cinderella," "Les Sylphides," "Yesterday's Spring," "The Tale of The Tsar-Sultan," "Light and Shadow," "First Ball," "Espanita," "Peter and The Wolf," "Pavlova's Solos," "Lincoln's Ladies," "Glass Harmonica," "Walpurgis Night."

Penelope Lagios, Gene Marinachio in "Swan Lake"
Above: Josefa Villanueva, Benjamin Reyes,
Ludmilla Bogart (R) in "Giselle". Top: Josefa Villanueva,
Benjamin Reyes in "Giselle"

"Coppelia"
Left: Merriem Lanova

161

BALLET CONCERTO
Miami, Florida

Directors, Sonia Diaz Blanco, Martha Del Pino; Scenery, Cecilio Noble; Costumes, Rene Sanchez.

PRINCIPAL DANCERS: Lydia Diaz Cruz, Alexander Nigodoff

COMPANY: Mariana Alvarez, Addy Azcarreta, Virginia Bari, Elsa Barros, Gretchen Bergstresser, Silvia Blanco, Zeida Cecilia, Charlene Gehm, Maria Gonzalez, Haydee Gutierrez, Leticia Medero, Manon Nunez, Rita Rudner, Susan Stadler, Michele Thorne, Hilda Maria Torres, Jill Van Arsdel, Gilberto Almaguer, Luis Arias, Jose Gomez, Gaby Henriquez, Mary Anson, Maria Flores, Patricia Penenori, Rene Sanchez, Bernard Zemble, Maria Cristina Torres, Fernando Bujones

REPERTOIRE: "Les Sylphides," "The Nutcracker," "Latin American Symphony," "Evocacion," "Romance," "Pas De Deux from Don Quixote," "Autumn," "Summer," second act of "Swan Lake" and "Giselle," "Las Bodas de Luis Alonso," "Death Of A Swan."

Marcel Studio and Phelan Photos

Lydia Diaz Cruz, Roberto Dimitrievitch, Manon Nunez in "Les Sylphides". Above: Lydia Diaz Cruz, Alexander Nigodoff in "Evocacion"

162

Lydia Diaz Cruz, Roberto Dimitrievitch in "Latin American Symphony"
Above: "Las Bodas De Luis Alonso"
Top: Sonia Diaz Blanco, Martha Del Pino

BALLET ETUDES REPERTORY COMPANY
Norwalk, Connecticut

Russel Fratto, Founder-Director; Jeanette Lauret, Co-Director; Resident Choreographer, Charles Nicoll; Ballet Mistress, Rosetta Newton; Managing Director, Robert Mowery; Associate Director, James Zynda.

PRINCIPAL DANCERS: Nancee Charles, Karen Williamson, James Zynda

COMPANY: Judith Czegledi, Mary La Monica, Jonsie Brough, Charles Nicoll, Anthony Germano, Virginia Horan, Darlene Rothbert, Jeffery Bentley, George Perez, Dennis Seeto, Janet Murray, Candace Cunningham, Linda Vospalek, Kathleen Craig, Jessica Hammond, Linda Fischer, Tommy Moore, Thomas Thompson, Mary Nardi, Elizabeth Stone, Kathleen Symanko, Shari Walk, Elizabeth Zisek.

REPERTOIRE (1965-66 Season): "Cinderella," "The Skaters," "Coppelia."

Mira Photos

James Zynda, Nancee Charles in "Coppelia"
Above: Jeannette Lauret

James Zynda, Nancee Charles
Above: "The Skaters". Top: "Cinderella"

Melissa Hayden, Jacques D'Amboise
in
"Stars And Stripes Pas De Deux"

BALLET SPECTACULAR
Miami, Florida

Conceived, Created, and Directed by Francis Mayville; Conductors, Kenneth Schermerhorn, Dean Ryan; Public Relations, A. Robert Owens; Stage Manager, Erick Santamaria.

A program of Pas de Deux and Pas de Trois performed by America's finest ballet artists.

ARTISTS: Jacques D'Amboise, Melissa Hayden, Allegra Kent, Lupe Serrano, Scott Douglas, Mimi Paul, Marina Svetlova, Oleg Briansky, Rochelle Zide, Ramon Segarra, George Zoritch, Patricia Neary, Frank Ohman.

REPERTOIRE (1965-66 season): Swan Lake (Act II), Les Sylphides, Giselle Pas de Deux (Act I), Meditation from "Thais" (Choreography, Jacques D'Amboise), Don Quixote Pas de Deux, Spring Waters, Black Swan Pas de Deux, Giselle (Act II), Blue Bird Pas de Deux, Stars and Stripes Pas de Deux, Dying Swan, Mendelssohn Pas de Deux, Sleeping Beauty Pas de Deux, Nutcracker Pas de Deux, Sylvia Pas de Deux, Tschaikovsky Pas de Deux, Coppelia Wedding Pas de Deux, Swan Lake Pas de Deux (Act II), Glazounov Pas de Deux, Le Corsaire, Ribbon Dance (Red Poppy), Raymonda Variations, Afternoon Of A Faun (Jerome Robbins), Pas de Deux from Pas de Dix, La Fille Mal Gardee Pas de Deux, Five Pieces, Cinderella Pas de Deux, World Premiere of Pas de Trois '20's (Choreography, Jacques D'Amboise), Raymonda Pas de Deux, Night Shadow, Le Combat, Irish Fantasy.

Martha Swope Photo

Mimi
Paul

George
Zoritch

Allegra Kent
Above: Rochelle Zide, Ramon Segarra

165

Jack Mitchell Photo

Scott Douglas, Lupe Serrano
in
"The Nutcracker Pas De Deux"
Ballet Spectacular

THE BALLET GUILD OF CLEVELAND
Cleveland, Ohio

Co-Artistic Directors, John Begg, Alex Martin; Associate Director and Repetiteur, John Williams; Maitresse de Ballet, Sandra Sykora; Designer, Morgan Rendell; Coutouriere, Irene Csatho; Musical Director, Bruce McIntyre; Choreographers, John Begg, William Dollar, Joan Hartshorne, Alex Martin, Mark Ryder.

COMPANY: Barbara Bozeman, Linda Bushnell, Linda Cady, Lisa Coffey, Jacqueline Gill, Judith Jaffa, Cynthia Maxwell, Susan McGuire, Paula Moller, Sharon Patterson, Helene Riggs, Audrey Soltesz, Karane Stoneman, Susan Stranahan, Sandra Sykora, Charee Walleck, Jean Winters, Kathleen Zamec, D'Vina Zimmerman, John Williams

REPERTOIRE (1965-66 Season): "Brandenburg Concerto," "The Nutcracker," "La Ronde," "Nocturne," "Roundelay," "Divertimento," "Pas De Trois," "The Fourth Adviser," "Three Dances For J.N.," "Coppelia" (Act III), "Concerto."

Edwin C. Perry Photos

"Three Dances For J. N.". Above: Karane Stoneman in "Coppelia". Top: John Williams, Christina Henley in "Coppelia"

Sandra Sykora, John Williams in "The Fourth Adviser". Above: Sandra Sykora, Karane Stoneman, Judith Jaffa, Charee Walleck in "La Ronde"

167

BOSTON BALLET COMPANY
Boston, Massachusetts
Second Season

E. Virginia Williams, Founder and Artistic Director; Artistic Adviser, George Balanchine; Executive Director, Ruth G. Harrington; Ballet Mistress, Sydney Leonard.

Sunday, December 19, 1965.
PROGRAM: Two performances of "The Nutcracker" with Maria Tallchief as guest artist, and Arthur Fiedler conducting.

Monday, January 17, 1966.
PROGRAM: World Premiere of "Time + 6" (Choreography, Anna Sokolow; Music, Teo Macero), "Napoli" (Choreography, Bournonville; Set by Hans Brenaa) with Warren Lynch and Carol Ravich, "Allegro Brillante" (Choreography, Balanchine; Music, Tschaikowsky) with guest artists Sara Leland and Earle Sieveling, who also danced the Grand Pas De Deux from "Stars and Stripes" (Balanchine/Sousa).

Monday, February 7, 1966.
PROGRAM: "Les Sylphides," "Perilous Time," "The Prodigal Son" with guest artists Edward Villella and Patricia Neary, who also danced "Donizetti Variations."

Sunday, March 20, 1966.
PROGRAM: World Premiere of "Stephen Foster Suite" (Choreography, E. Virginia Williams; Music by Foster), "The Combat" with Melissa Hayden and Conrad Ludlow, who were joined by Sara Leland in "Serenade," "Pastorale" (Moncion).

Photos by Studio 350, Alfred Schroeder and Jack Mitchell

Carol Ravich, Laura Young, Linda Di Bona, Ellen O'Reilly in "Pas De Quatre".
Above: Earle Sieveling, Sara Leland
Top: E. Virginia Williams

Patricia Neary, Edward Villella in "Prodigal Son"

Cynthia Heaton, Stephen Wistrich, Ellen O'Reilly, Robert Pierce in "Time + 6"
Above: "Concerto Barocco". Top: (L) Carol Ravich, Robert Pierce
(R) Anthony Williams, Ellen O'Reilly in "Napoli"

THE CAROLINA BALLET
Columbia, South Carolina

Lanneau Foster, Director; Margaret Foster, Ballet Mistress and Choreographer; Artistic Adviser, Decor and Costume Designer, Catherine Rembert; Dottie Dreiman, Makeup Chairman.

COMPANY: Linda Baroody, Dale Brown, Roseann Bultman, Anne Cameron, Donna Church, Carl Crosby, Betty Darden, Bettina Derrick, David Dreiman, Evelyn Ellis, Linda Entzminger, Lynn Ficken, Pixie Foster, Peter Garrick, Mickey Mattox, Susan Dale Patterson, Gerry Patterson, Rose Anne Rivkin, Carrington Salley, Polly Anna Smith, Lilly Stern, Gail Thomas, Helen Tilton, Faye Ward, Joan E. Watkins.

REPERTOIRE: "Swan Lake," "Gypsy Baron," "Jeux D'Enfants," "College Vignettes," "Lyric Interlude," "Overtures," "Les Sylphides," "The Seasons," "Prince Igor," "Carnaval," "Coppelia," "Les Patineurs," "Bolero," "Fantasy," "Raymonda," "Roumanian Rhapsody," "Ballet Egyptian," "Tartaran de Tarascon," "Western Jazz," "Peter Pan," "The Nutcracker," "Aurora's Wedding," "Cinderella," "The Velvet Sombrero," "Beauty and The Shepherd," "Graduation Ball," "The Shoemaker and The Fairy."

Catherine Rembert
Above: Lanneau
L. Foster

Betty Darden,
Carl Crosby

CHARLESTON CIVIC BALLET
Charleston, West Virginia

Andre Van Damme, Founder-Director; Stanley Zompakos, Artistic Director, Choreographer, and Designer.

SOLOISTS: Cathy Buchanan, Helen Cannon, Don Cantwell, Edward Douglas, Kathy Gianaris, Sharon Kennedy, Elizabeth Pitts, Susan Rush, Peter Theos

REPERTOIRE: "Divertissement," "Imago," "Nocturne," "Visions Fugitives," "Psyche and Eros," "Pavanne," "Four Episodes," "Holberg Suite," "Soirees," "Cycle," "Impressions," "Printemps," "Pulchinella," "The End Game," "Etude," "Tilt!," "Pas De Quatre," "The Guest," "Amoretto," "Blanc et Noire," "Contrasts," "Electronic Etude," "The Exorcism," "Melodic Configurations," "Pot Pourri," "Ritual," "Fancy Regale."

Susan Rush, Peter Theos, Don Cantwell, Sharon Kennedy, Elizabeth Pitts in "The Guest". Above: Stanley Zompakos Right: Don Cantwell, Bilbro, Edward Douglas, Sharon Kennedy in "Pas De Quatre"

CHAUTAUQUA DANCE COMPANY
Chautauqua, N. Y.

Statia Sublette, Founder, Director, and Choreographer.

COMPANY: Statia Sublette, Paul Hangauer, John Crespo, Kenneth Collins, Diane Lewis, Pamela Geracci, Carol Karver, Mary Sue Finnerty, Nancy Gregory, Bobbi Jo Baumann, Kathy Bricher, Susan Morton, Holly Fliegler, Mary Jane Eisenberg, Susan Lelden, Sandra Bebell, Carol Kravec, Deborah Bradt, Andrea Matujasic, Octavine Swanson.

REPERTOIRE: "Peter and The Wolf," "Waltz Of The Flowers," "Gather Round For a Hootenanny," "Straussian Suite," "This Is Ballet."

Mary Jane Eisenberg, Paul Hangauer, Kathleen Bricher, Bobbi Jo Baumann, John Daly King, Sandra Bebell, Statia Sublette in "Straussian Suite"

COLUMBUS BALLET GUILD
Columbus, Georgia

Artistic Director and Choreographer, Rossie Gilmore; Assistant Director, Vic Prophet; Costumes, Carolyn Alexander.

COMPANY: Carolyn Alexander, Cheryl Bush, Glynne Gilmore, Susan Lotz, Vicki Morales, Ingo Orlamunder, Jane Spivey, Christy Weaver, Irene Alexich, Jim Burke, Merrilyn Krider, Pat MacMurrain, Shelley Noble, Vic Prophet, Stephanie Stenberg, Barbara Wein

REPERTOIRE (1965-66 Season): "Waltz from Sleeping Beauty," "On A Dark Night," "Dance Macabre," "El Amor Brujo," "The Eye Of the Beholder," "Divertissement."

Vicki Morales, Byron Grant in "The Eye Of The Beholder" Above: Rossie Gilmore. Right: Vicki Morales, Jim Burke, Shelley Noble in "Classical Ballet"

DALLAS CIVIC BALLET
Dallas, Texas

Artistic Adviser, Nathalie Krassovska; Choreographers, Jerry Bywaters Cochran, Denise Lattes Brown; Company Manager, Denise Brown; Stage Manager, Patricia Hyde; Director, Don Cranford; Conductor, Donald Johanos; Settings, Peter Wolf; Costumes, Lorene Head, Alice Watkins.

GUEST ARTISTS: Nathalie Krassovska, Nancy Schaffenburg, Victor Moreno, Fernando Schaffenburg

COMPANY: Anette Brown, Patti Thompson, Christi Curtis, Debrah King-Riggs, Pam Thornton, Colleen Saville, Suzanne Cranford, Linda Spiritas, Candace Jones, Laura Pierce, Nancy Griffith, Susan Wells, Linda Noltmeier, Tish Skelton, Marjorie Kovich, Zach Ward, Denny Poole, Bobbie Heath, Lana Nelson, Byneta Head, Ann Reitman, Betty Williams, Pam Peadon, Barbara Berkeley, Averille Browning, Dana Dorman, Laurie Harris, Patty Hartley, Cathy Pierce, Renee Reese, Suzanne Scott, Becky Smith, Ann Yonack, Carol Willis, Ann Reitman, Celeste Ward, Happy Thigpen, Steve Riley, Dale Riley, Jeff Butler, Andre Danwill, Phil Johnson, Bobby Heath, Lorraine Cranford

REPERTOIRE (1965-66 Season): "The Nutcracker," "Alaskan Totem Pole Dance," "Nova Scotian Sword Dance," "Brazilian Rhumba," "American Cakewalk," "Ballet Court," "Suite Francaise," "Mexican Folk Dances," "Pas De Trois from Swan Lake," "The Unicorn, The Gorgon and The Manticore."

Right: Nathalie Krassovska in "Waltz Of The Flowers". Above: Nathalie Krassovska, Victor Moreno, Jerry Bywaters Cochran

Debra King-Riggs, Happy Thigpen, Laura Pierce in "The Nutcracker"

"The Unicorn, The Gorgon And The Manticore" Above: Laura Pierce, Anette Brown, Candace Jones, Christi Curtis, Lorraine Cranford in "Unicorn"

172

DANCE WEST
San Francisco, California

Jenny Hunter, Director and Choreographer.

COMPANY: Jenny Hunter, Margaret Hill, Ann McClaughry, Ann Swearingen, Jane Lapiner, Paula Chertok, Amelia Silver, Bill McClaughry, Seth Hill, Jeani Nagy, Belinda Ricklefs

REPERTOIRE: "Quick Song," "Seren," "Solo With Figures," "Epilogue: The Saturday Dance," "The Echo-Surprise," "Parsec," "Riddle," "Stroll," "Places Without Names."

Phil Mozesson Photo

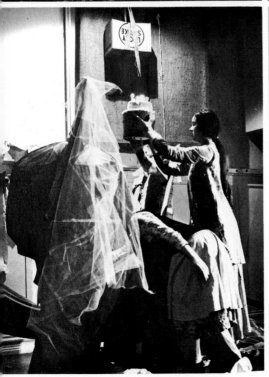

Jenny Hunter, Ann McClaughry, Seth Hill, Margaret Hill in "Epilogue: The Saturday Dance" Above: Jane Lapiner, Jenny Hunter, Paula Chertok, Amelia Silva in "The Echo—Surprise Dance"

Margaret Hill, Ann McClaughry, Jenny Hunter in "Places Without Names". Above: Ann McClaughry, Ann Swearingen, Jane Lapiner in "Riddle". Top: Jenny Hunter as The Nightingale

DANCE INCORPORATED CHICAGO
Chicago, Illinois

Gus Giordano, Founder, Director, Choreographer; Judith Scott, Associate Director; Ronald Colton, Ballet Master.

COMPANY: Gus Giordano, Judith Scott, Gary Kaplan, Mort Kessler, Rita Rojas

REPERTOIRE: "American Jazz Trilogy," "The Garden," "Vagaries," "Kontakte," "The West Side," "The Jazz Drum," "Menage."

From top: Mort Kessler, Gary Kaplan, Gus Giordano in "Menage". Above: Judith Scott in "Kontakte"

From top: Mort Kessler, Rita Rojas, Gary Kaplan, Judith Scott, Gus Giordano. Above: Gus Giordano

174

Rebecca Wright, Jon Rodriguez
in "Dance Overture"

Nancy Baker, Margaret Dawson, Doreen Roche,
David Blackburn, Diana Mileski in "Night Soliloquies"

Jack Mitchell Photo

DAYTON CIVIC BALLET
Dayton, Ohio

Founder, Artistic Director, Choreographer, Josephine Schwarz; Ballet Master, Choreographer, David McLain; Wardrobe Mistress, Karolyn Ziegler.

COMPANY: David Blackburn, Jenni Daly, Cynthia Deane, Danny Duell, Kristin Elliott, Vicki Garlitz, Tim Graves, Celia Ipiotis, Nancy Johnson, Diana Mileski, Jo Neiman, Jon Rodriguez, Stuart Sebastian, Debra Snyder, Paul Sprague, Katherine Walker, David Weaver, Rebecca Wright, Joyce Ziegler

REPERTOIRE (1965-66 Season): "The Nutcracker," "Grand Pas De Deux from The Nutcracker," "Blue Bird Pas De Deux from Sleeping Beauty," "Pas De Quatre," "Dance Overture," "New York (A Creative Process)," "Night Soliloquy," "I Watched Myself Grow Up," "Birthday Of The Infanta."

Walt Kleine Photo

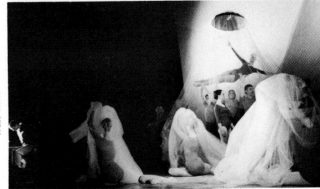

Premiere of "New Work". Above: Joyce Ziegler,
Robert Thoma in "Dance Overture"
Left: Josephine Schwartz

175

DANCERS' WORKSHOP COMPANY
San Francisco, California

Ann Halprin, Director; Members of Company perform, compose, collaborate, and direct all the arts into a total synthesis.

COMPANY: Larry Goldsmith, Paul Goldsmith, John Graham, Kim Hahn, Ann Halprin, Patrick Hickey, Jo Landor, A. A. Leath, Daria Lurie, Jani Novak, Folke Rabe, Charles Ross, Rana Schuman, Morton Subotnick

PROGRAM (1965-66 Season): "Parades and Changes."

Below and right:
Dancers' Workshop Company

Mme. Halina

Ramon Segarra
Above: (C) Eleanor D'Antuono, Ramon Segarra in "The Nutcracker"

ELMIRA-CORNING BALLET COMPANY
Elmira, New York

Mme. Halina, Founder, Artistic Director, Choreographer; Conductor, Theodore Hollenbach; Choreographer-Teacher, Rochelle Zide.

GUEST ARTISTS: Eleanor D'Antuono, Ramon Segarra

COMPANY: Deborah Boughton, Karen Larson, Robert Crocker, Suzanne Gush, Eleanor Shaw, Sharon Rubinski, Cynthia Doty, Gail Erway, Dolores Leach, Kitty Sirp, William Worden, Terri Hall, Linda Weale, Louise Richardson, Victoria Jenkins, Barbara Fisher, Pamela Winnick, Daniel Waldo, Marlene Misnick, Mary Alice Trescott, Ginger Fancher, Candase Doty, Susan Meltzer.

REPERTOIRE (1965-66 Season): "The Nutcracker," "Swan Lake," "Masquerade."

FLINT BALLET THEATRE
Flint, Michigan

Artistic Director, Choreographer, Lena Pelio; Musical Director, Raymond Gerkowski; Assistant Co-Directors, James Paavola, Jackie Paul; Choreographers, Robert Lunnon, Osvald Lemanis, Dom Orjudeos.

GUEST ARTISTS: Doreen Tempest, Robert Lunnon

COMPANY: Barbara Church, Jackie Paul, James Paavola, Kay McCarty, Sandra Ochodnicky, Marilyn Kaercher, Louetta Rice, Sandra Hogue, Jacqueline Paul, Lee Paavola, Ronnie Brown, Mike Shortall, Linda Novak, Tania Fedchenko, Roseanne Thomas, Linda Karsoe, Lori Slocum

REPERTOIRE (1965-66 Season): "Cinderella," "Seasons," "Competition," "Swan Lake," "The Magic Jewelry Box," "Snow White," "Warsaw Concert In Jazz," "Sleeping Beauty," "Bartered Bride."

Hicks and Smith Photos

Tania Fedchenko, Barbara Church, Linda Rhoads, Sue Adams in "Swan Lake". Above: James Paavola, Barbara Church in "Graduation Ball" Top: (L) Jane Pilon, Louetta Rice, Gaye Palinsky in "Competition". (R) Lena Pelio

Dan Durkacy, Sandra Ochodnicky in "Carnaval" Above: James Paavola, Mary Lane in "Seasons" Top: James Paavola, Kay McCarty in "Swan Lake"

FORT WORTH BALLET ASSOCIATION
Fort Worth, Texas

Fernando Schaffenburg, Artistic Director and Choreographer; Nancy Schaffenburg, Artistic Adviser; Rhyna Headrick, Regisseur; Letitia Gray, Assistant Ballet Mistress; Rudolph Kruger, Musical Director.

GUEST ARTISTS: Fernando and Nancy Schaffenburg, Victor Moreno.

SOLOISTS: Margaret Moar, Margo Dean, Linda Baldridge, Eileen Fritz, Kay Ledbetter, Barbara Macklem, Jo Ann Oldt.

CORPS DE BALLET: Sheri Abraham, Sharon E. Bahr, Linda Bryan, Claire Dishongh, Gail Dorflinger, Marilyn Dye, Lovie Fleishman, Marilyn Gaston, Jan Haley, Sherry Kornitsky, Gayle Kassing, Mary Lynn Lewis, Marilyn MacKinder, Janice Minshew, Vicki Nadolski, Cherry Tompkins, Margaret van der Vliet, Sharon Vaughan, Jon Cheetwood, Bobby Heath, Barbara Sims, Cathy Smart.

REPERTOIRE (1965-66 Season): "Les Sylphides," "Grand Pas De Deux from The Nutcracker," "Interlude," "Caracol."

Barbara Macklem, Fernando Schaffenburg in "Interlude". Above: Linda Baldridge (R), Barbara Macklem (L) in "Caracol"

"Interlude". Above: Victor Moreno in "Les Sylphides" Top: Nancy and Fernando Schaffenburg in "The Nutcracker"

GARDEN STATE BALLET
Newark, N. J.

Fred Danieli, Founder, Artistic Director, and Choreographer.

SOLOISTS: Marjorie Spohn, Julia Frederick, Ramon Segarra, Veronika Mlakar, Linda DiBona, Warren Lynch

REPERTOIRE: "Introduction To Ballet," "Pas De Quatre," "Divertimento," "11x11x11," "Nutcracker Pas De Deux," "Symphony In C" (First Movement), "Four Cantos," "Stephen Foster Suite."

Left: Julia Frederick and corps de ballet
in "Symphony In C"
Garden State Ballet

ILLINOIS BALLET
Chicago, Illinois

Directors, Richard Ellis, Christine DuBoulay; Associate Director and Resident Choreographer, Dom Orejudos; Choreographers, Sir Frederick Ashton, Ray Powell, Eric Braun, George Montaign, Dom Orejudos, Hy Somers; Technical Director, William Ploeger; Musical Adviser, William Hughes.

COMPANY: Dom Orejudos, Christine DuBoulay, Pamela Johnson, Samyiel Kurkjian, Walter Kaiser, Daiva Gestautas, Juanita Lopez, Vera Rast, Siga Zymantas, Jock Abra, Helga Schulz, Paula Vandenberg, Gemma Apley, Ronald Federico, Richard Ellis, Elisabeth Herskind

REPERTOIRE (1965-66 Season): "Con Gioco" (Montaign/von Dohnanyi), "This Present Image" (Prokofieff/Orejudos), "The Fifth and Briefest Season" (Orejudos/Balazs), "Facade" (Ashton/Walton).

Pamela Johnson, Dom Orejudos in "Giselle"
Left: Richard Ellis, Christine DuBoulay

179

LOS ANGELES FESTIVAL BALLET
Los Angeles, California

Eva Lorraine, Founder, Artistic Director, and Choreographer.

COMPANY: Ellen Buchea, Bruce Bain, Edgar Johnson, Cindy Peacock, Charthel Arthur, Paula Muller, Jody Aaen, Nadine Cavaleri, Tom Sanders, Darlene Gillespie, Carole Elkins, Darlene Reed, Charles Fernald, Ardis Conant, Joan Conant, Pamela Conant, Linda Bower, Gina Gillespie, Larianne Gillespie, Darlene Gillespie

REPERTOIRE: "Concerto," "Galatea," "Boccaccio," "The Firebird," "Black Swan Pas De Deux," "Western Symphony," "Les Sylphides," "Command Performance," "Rhapsody In Blue," "Salute U.S.A."

John E. Reed Photo

LOS ANGELES "JR" BALLET
Beverly Hills, California

Irina Kosmovska, Artistic Director and Choreographer; Wardrobe Coordinator, Suzanne Bittner; Lighting, Alice Nishimura; Stage Manager, Jo McMahan; Guest Choreographer, David Lichine.

GUEST ARTISTS: Don Hewitt, Laszlo Jilly, William Tarpy

SOLOISTS: Victoria Hathaway, Leslie Kimble, Greg Kimble, Jeannie Samuel, Kevyn O'Rourke.

REPERTOIRE: "Chopin Concerto No. 1," "Classical Symphony," "Coppelia," "Graduation Ball," "Greetings From Vienna," "La Creation," "Magic Bonnet," "Nutcracker Suite," "Red Shoes," "Schubert Impromptus," "Sleeping Beauty," "Swan Lake" (Act II), "Ugly Duckling," "The Ballerina and The Clown," "The Tarantella."

Los Angeles "JR" Ballet in Hollywood Bowl
Above: Tom Sandars, Carole Elkins, and right:
Eva Lorraine of Los Angeles Festival Ballet

McLEAN BALLET COMPANY
McLean, Virginia

Thera Grefe, Artistic Director nnd Choreographer; Stephan Mucsi, Ballet Master and Choreographer; Peter Jamerson, Production Manager.

COMPANY: Natalie Almy, Yorke Brown, Gerda Enderli, Donna Indyke, William Martin, Gloria McLean, Edward Myers, Kathy Northern, Susan Pistorino, Steven Shipman, Vera M. Smith, Laurie Trayhern, Gregg Wilson

REPERTOIRE: "Annabelle," "Etc.," "Snow White," "Youth Concerto," "Hungarian Gypsy Holiday."

Shirley Nottingham Photos

Donna Indyke, Edward Myers in "Snow White"
Above: Gregg Wilson in
"Hungarian Gypsy Holiday"

Gregg Wilson, Steve Shipman, Gerda Enderli,
Gloria McLean in "Hungarian Gypsy Holiday"
Above: Guest Doris Wood Murphy in "Don Quixote"
Top: Gregg Wilson, Kathy Northern, Dawn Miller,
Laurie Trayhern in "Youth Concerto"

181

THE MIAMI BALLET
Miami, Florida

Thomas Armour, Artistic Director; Choreographer, Designer, Ballet Master, Robert Pike; Renee Zintgraff, Director of Junior Company; Carmen Nappo, Composer-Conductor.

SOLOISTS: Wendy Mallory, Paula Mallory, Kathleen Essex, Karen Anderson, Carol Sue Cuppy, Jeanine LeMire, Garielle Whittle, Carmen Mendez, Mindy Gars, Phil Hoffman, George Vargas, Kurt Nagle, Eugenia Vachon, Colleen Sullivan, Patricia Strauss, Mary Fellman, Robert Pike, Renee Zintgraff, Kathleen Essex, Laura Rose May

REPERTOIRE (1965-66 Season): "Black and White," "Ballet De La Jeunesse," "Americans In Paris," "Swan Lake," "Pas De Trois," "Entr'Acte," "Frontier Town," "Aida."

Left: Robert Pike, Mary Fellman
Below: Thomas Armour, Renee Zintgraft
Bottom: Carol Sue Cuppy, Paula Mallory,
Wendy Mallory, Jo Wanda Grace
The Miami Ballet

MISSISSIPPI COAST BALLET
Gulfport, Mississippi

Delia Stewart, Artistic Director and Choreographer; Costumes, Mrs. H. E. Ward; Lighting, Jay Cooper; Stage Manager, Arthur Muhleisen.

GUEST ARTIST: Lloyd Labit

SOLOISTS: Clare Weddington, Lynell Langston, Merrilly Bertucci, Linda Granger, Ronny Cumberland, David Cummins, Frank Gill, Barry Kalinauslas, Mary Smith, Patty Miller, Delia Stewart

REPERTOIRE: "Les Sylphides," "Slaughter On Tenth Avenue," "The Jewel and The Lotus."

Delia Stewart
Mississippi Coast Ballet

MINNEAPOLIS CONTEMPORARY DANCE THEATER
Minneapolis, Minnesota

Loyce Houlton, Artistic Director and Choreographer; David Voss, Musical Director; John Donahue, Technical Director; Costumes, Mildred Bullock; Ballet Mistress, Victoria Christenson.

COMPANY: Marcia Halmers, Andrea Schulberg, Phyllis Patalas, Frances Machala, Marsha Longstaff, David Voss, Larry DeVries, Peter Hauschild, Robert Crabb, Daniel Seagren

REPERTOIRE: "Vagaries," "Epitaphs and Enigmas," "The Nutcracker Fantasy," "The Little Match Girl," "Concertpiece," "When You Are Not Homely, You Don't Have To Spend Every Night With A Book!," "Metamorphosis," "Haiku," "Variations," "Sylvan Misadventures," "Ecliptus," "A Baroque Soiree," "Mass," "Dialogues," "Ritual," "Folksay," "Opus, Jazz!"

Below: Larry De Vries, Frances Machala in "Symphony In C". Right: with Robert Crabb in "Vagaries" Below: Marsha Longstaff

Peter Marcus Photos

Cathy Rice, Karen Redder, Linda Gray, Barbara Elias, Judy Premus, Bonnie Rapp, Joyce Whitman, Maryann Simonson, Bernedette Poje in "Shubertania"

NEWBURGH BALLET GUILD
Newburgh, New York

Artistic Directors and Choreographers, Fred de Mayo, Marya Kennett; Sets, Richard Jones; Lighting, Ben Seidman; Costumes, Olive Pearson.

PRINCIPAL ARTISTS: Barbara Ellias, Claude Noel, Marya Kennett, Fred de Mayo

CORPS DE BALLET: Linda Gray, Jeanne Hutchins, Bonnie Rapp, Jean Schmid, Bernadette Poje, Michele Wilson, Virginia Strong, Lynn Pearson, Ellen Keller, Karen Furno, Claudia McHugh, Eileen Bellizzi, Valerie McGinnis, Paula Cussick, Nancy Jackson, Margo Scalzi, Carol Michaluk, Robert O'Dell, Joseph Mazzello, Karen Redder, Meg Pessin, Judy Premus, Barbara McCargo, Hanna Tagashige, Joyce Whitman, Lava Redfield, Joanne White, Laurie Shesa, Linda Zaworski, Tom Gibney, John Barone, Edward Carroll

REPERTOIRE: "Shubertania," "Variations To Concerto," "Ballet Mistress," "The Piper Plays," "Orchestre Vivant."

RUTH PAGE'S CHICAGO OPERA AND INTERNATIONAL BALLET
Chicago, Illinois

Director-Choreographer, Ruth Page; Assistant Director, Kenneth Johnson; Ballet Master, Larry Long; Regisseur, Donald Judge; Company Manager, Phillipe de Conville; Press, Marilynn LeVine; Musical Adaptations, Isaac Van Grove; Conductor, Simon Sadoff.

GUEST STARS: Irina Borowska, Karl Musil, Kirsten Simone, Henning Kronstam, Anton Dolin

PRINCIPAL DANCERS: Patricia Klekovic, Kenneth Johnson, Orrin Kayan, Dolores Lipinski, Larry Long, Charles Schick, Jeanne Armin

SOLOISTS: Judith Thelen, John Landowski, Vicki Fisera, Audrey Deckmann

CORPS DE BALLET: Esther Adelman, Jeanne Ocasek, Sarah Wisdom, Violetta Karosas, Raya Lee, Lynne Kirk, Mary McIntosh, Madeleine Camston, Sharon Schensky, Alan Kirk, Paul Krumm, Barry Edson, David Milnes, Bud Heidebur, Harvey Hysell, Madeleine Rozak, Birute Barodicaite, Anna Baker, Sarah Jane Smith, Judie Ann Sodini, Gerre Cimino, Marie Laurence Bonnet, Lloyd Labit, Richard Lichter, Jerry Kent, Jose Valenzuela, Richard Arve

REPERTOIRE (1965-66 Season): "The Nutcracker," "Carmen," "The Merry Widow," "Camille," "Die Fledermaus," "Combinations," "Mephistophela," "Bullets or Bon-Bons," and pas de deux from "Swan Lake," "Flower Festival," "Don Quixote," "Sleeping Beauty," "Idylle," "Bagatelles."

Left: Ruth Page

Patricia Klekovic, Kenneth Johnson
in "Carmen"

Jeanne Armin, Orrin Kayan
in "Combinations"

Irina Borowska
Above and top: "The Nutcracker"

Jeanne Armin and corps in "Bullets Or Bon-Bons"
Above: Jeanne Armin, Charles Schick in "Walpurgis"

PREMIERE DANCE ARTS COMPANY
Denver, Colorado

Gwen Bowen, Artistic Director and Choreographer; Sets and Lighting, Henry Lowenstein, Kathleen Caldwell.

GUEST ARTIST: Dean Crane

COMPANY: Kathy Adam, Linda Arnold, Penny Jensen, Valerie Hammer, Deborah Goldsmith, Christine Weidman, Vicki Moritz, Debbie Norblom, Melody Youmans, Elaine Lenhart, Rick Eddy, Dixie Locklin, Sylvia Plett, Deborah Smith, Diane Herbst, Cora-Lee Lynnock, Merrelyn Miller, Leo Robertson, Valerie Marrese, Corliss Kirby, Jan Goodman, Deanne Beal, Diane Herbst, Corliss Kirby, Kathrine Linstedt, Peggy Oliver

REPERTOIRE (1965-66 Season): Scenes from "The Bartered Bride," "Tosca," "Cavalleria," and "Prince Igor," "The Web," "Bach," "Beethoven," "Nowhere To Now," "The Ugly Duckling," "The Nutcracker Suite," "La Boutique Fantasque."

Smyth Studio Photo

Gwen Bowen, Dean Crane
in "Tosca"

Cliff Jensen, Dixie Locklin, Peter Monette
in "Bartered Bride". Above Kathy Adam (C) in
"The Ugly Duckling"

Albert Guise Photos

Richard Armour, Michael Tevlin,
Suzanne Rowland in "The Fortune Teller"
Right: Stanley Herbertt, Kathleen Kornfeld,
Phyllis Roberts

ST. LOUIS CIVIC BALLET
St. Louis, Missouri

Stanley Herbertt, Artistic Director and Resident Choreographer; LaVerne Meyering, Ballet Mistress.

SOLOISTS: Kathleen Kornfeld, Carole Logaglio, Susan Checkett, Suzanne Rowland, Michael Tevlin, Richard Armour, Christine Knoblauch, Marsha Rubin, Richard Darrough, Phyllis Roberts

CORPS DE BALLET: Christine Bohlman, Renee Baughman, Cheri Lagana, Rita Roberts, Lise Hoffman, Judy Jostrand, Phyllis Smith, Andrea Jacobs, Penny Rieser, Sandra Hare, Kristine Karwoski, Patricia Middleton, Milamarie Olds, Donna Prunkard, Karen Sanders, Cheryl Sobelman, Susan Stumpf, Pamela Tucker

REPERTOIRE (1965-66 Season): "The Fortune Teller," "L'Academie," "Gazebo," "Melodrama!"

Jillana
Guest Artist with San Diego Ballet

SAN DIEGO BALLET COMPANY
San Diego, California

Richard Carter, Artistic Director and Choreographer; Musical Adviser, James K. Guthrie; Technical Director, Bruce Kelley; Artistic Advisers, Lew Christensen, Eugene Loring.

GUEST ARTISTS: Maria Tallchief, Kent Stowell, Jillana, Nancy Johnson, Richard Carter

SOLOISTS: Jon Blake, Deborah Hadley, James Heaverlo, Maxine Mahon, Kitty Vallacher, Karen Hudak

CORPS DE BALLET: Diana Davis, Sherlyn Dierkop, Marlene Jennings, Hollis Trainer, Daniel Amick, Michael Straubinger, Barbara Martin, Patricia Doty, Barbara Fitzgerald, Marlene Jennings, Patrice Marks, Shawn Stuart, James Francis, Walter Pomeroy

REPERTOIRE (1965-66 Season): "Con Amore," "Romeo and Juliet," "Die Liebchen," "Simple Symphony," "Man, Woman, and Child," "A Masque of Beauty and The Shepherd," "The Dryad," "Una Dozzina," "Filling Station," "The Nutcracker," "Le Gourmand," "Classical Symphony," "A La Francaix," "Bach Suite," "Aubade," "Variations $8 + 2$," "Show-Case," "Swan Lake" (Act II), "Les Sylphides," "Renard," "Western Orpheus," "The Sisters," and pas de deux from "Don Quixote," "Blue Bird," "Nutcracker," "White Swan."

Nancy Johnson in "Romeo And Juliet"
Above: Richard Carter

Nancy Johnson, James Heaverlo
in "The Dryad"

Jon Blake, Deborah Hadley, James Francis
in "A La Francaix". Above: "Romeo And Juliet" Corps
Top: Hollis Trainer, Jon Blake in "Classical Symphony"

James Heaverlo in "Romeo And Juliet"
Above: Kent Stowell, Maria Tallchief

"Beauty And The Beast"
Above: "Concert Music For Strings And Brass"
San Francisco Ballet

SAN FRANCISCO BALLET
San Francisco, California

Lew Christensen, General Director and Choreographer; Conductors, Gerhard Samuel, Robert Hughes, Lawrence Foster; Leon Kalimos, Managing Director; Ballet Master, Carlos Carvajal.

COMPANY: David Anderson, Sally Bailey, Joan DeVere, Betsy Erickson, Robert Gladstein, Sue Lloyd, Lynda Meyer, Nancy Robinson, R. Clinton Rothwell, Jocelyn Vollmar, and Eloise Tjomsland, Lee Fuller, Bill Breedlove, Zola Dishong, Barbara Begany, Henry Berg, Frank Ordway, Virginia Johnson, Marolyn Gyorfi, Maureen Wiseman, Henry Kersh, Bill Johnson, Jon Engstrom, Julie Williams, Ann Worthington, Maile Ackerman, Ingrid Fraley, Sarah Maule, Christine Bennett, Patricia Garland, Wendy Holt, David Coll, John McFall, Carlos Carvajal, Tina Kalimos, Kerry Williams, Michael Sterns, Virgil Bishop, Uta Enders, Deanne Rowland, Katy Warner, Alan Bergman, John Patterson, Illana De Heurtaumont, Penelope Lagios, Kenneth Lipsitz, Salicia Smith, Jud Stoddard

REPERTOIRE (1965-66 Season): Premieres of "Concertino," "Peasant Pas De Deux," "Balletino," "Siempre Bach," "Way Out," "Libation," "Pas De Trois," "Song Without Words," "Defeat," "Highway 101," "Souvenir," "Hubgarica," "Real Games," "Reflections," "Showoff," "Face Of Death," "Alpenfest," "Wajang," "Scotch Symphony," and revivals of "Filling Station," "Original Sin," "Life," "Concert Music For Strings and Brass," "Beauty and The Beast," "The Nutcracker," "Divertissement D'Auber," "Sinfonia," "Shadows," "Variations de Ballet," and World Premieres of "Pas De Deux," and "Pas De Quatre."

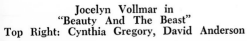

Jocelyn Vollmar in
"Beauty And The Beast"
Top Right: Cynthia Gregory, David Anderson

Sally Bailey, Robert Gladstein in "The Nutcracker"
Above: (L) Lew Christensen
(R) Marolyn Gyorfi, William Johnson

191

Lynda Meyer, David Anderson (C) with members of
San Francisco Ballet in "Life"

SAN FRANCISCO CONTEMPORARY DANCERS
San Francisco, California

J Marks, Choreographer-Director; Musical Director, Virgil Gonsalves; Scenic Designers, Roger Ferragallo, Robin Wagner; Costumes, James Croshaw; Lighting, J Marks; Stage Manager, Lynn Vardeman.

COMPANY: J Marks, James Croshaw, Diana Russell, Jean Mathis, Raymond Evans, Nancy Wolfe, Gayle Howard, Merry Barg, Helen Sanders, Michelle Sevryn, Harveyette Cohen, Sandra Viera, Sandra Shea, Mardi Van Winkle, Robert Crandall, Alan Vieau, Rudy Grau, Pat Finnegan, Barbara Keeling, Bruce Mack, Gary Pinely, Louis Roedhel

GUEST STARS: Alice Ghostley, Anita O'Day

REPERTOIRE (1965-66 Season): "Anna Karenina," "The Ceremony Of Innocence," "Saint Joan," "Desire," "Kama Sutras," "The Night Is A Sorceress," "A Season In Hell," "The Thurber Set," "Intermezzo," "Ravel Concerto," "Man and His Desire," "Oracle of The Branch," "Adagio," "The Miraculous Mandarin," "Roshomon," "Puppet Show For People," "Hallelujah!," "Biographies For Bugs," "Mother Was A Piltdown Man," "Love Is A Ball!"

Diana Russell, James Croshaw, Nancy Wolfe,
Raymond Evans in "Love Is A Ball!"
Left: Nancy Wolfe, James Croshaw
in "A Season In Hell"
San Francisco Contemporary Dancers

TOLEDO BALLET COMPANY
Toledo, Ohio

Marie Bollinger Vogt, Artistic Director and Choreographer; Resident Ballerina, Velta Cernonok.

COMPANY: Rusti Brandman, Polly Brandman, Sally Burgin, Marcia Beddoes, Gayle DeKany, Frances Gerken, Sue Henningsen, Jo Ann Johnon, Olivia Kallile, Nancy Gigliotti, Jan Millis, Jan Opperman, Terri Poland, Sharon Rumple, Karen Stanbery, Lora Lee Williams, Melissa Witzler, Mary Vascik, Harriet Zucker, Ernst Hillenbrand, Tony Pantoja, Sharon Russell, Debbie Cytrynowicz, Betsy Baron, Diane Bullano

REPERTOIRE (1965-66 Season): "The Nutcracker," "Aurora's Wedding," "Swan Lake," "Water Music," "Symphony For Fun," "American Dance Suite," "Kitty Kat Bird," "Les Sylphides," "Les Petits Riens," "A Night At Prince Orlovsky's," "Capriccio Espagnol," "Smorgasbord For Strings," "Old King Cole," "Les Patineurs," and Premiere of "Beautiful Toledo, Ohio."

Herral Long Photo

Members of Toledo Ballet

193

UTAH CIVIC BALLET
Salt Lake City, Utah

William F. Christensen, Artistic Director and Choreographer; Gordon Paxman, Associate Director; Bene Arnold, Ballet Mistress; Gary Horton, Production Associate; Keith Pippin, Stage Manager; Lynn Roseman, Lighting.

GUEST ARTISTS: Lupe Serrano, Scott Douglas

SOLOISTS: Anne Burton, Gary Horton, Shirley Nelson, Barbara Hamblin, Diane Cuatto, Vicki Chruma, Susan Smith, Peggy Scott, Kenneth Mitchell, Mary Ellen Davis, Diane Cole, Carolyn Smith, Leslie Grundman, Carol Nakamura, Rowland Butler, Ben Lokey, Richard Tanner

REPERTOIRE: "Con Amore," "Pas de Six," "Serenade," Premiere of "The Creatures of Prometheus," "Swan Lake" (Act II), "Coppelia," "La Valse," Premiere of "Badinage," "Romeo and Juliet."

Clayton Photos

Gary Horton, Anne Burton in "Romeo And Juliet"
Above: Diane Cole, Carolyn Smith, Ben Lokey, Leslie Grundman, Rowland Butler, Carol Nakamura, Richard Tanner in "The Creatures Of Prometheus"

Anne Burton, Gary Horton in "Swan Lake"
Top Left: "La Valse"

VALENTINA OUMANSKY DRAMATIC DANCE ENSEMBLE
Van Nuys, California

Director and Choreographer, Valentina Oumansky; Costumes, Rosalie Utterback, Taeko.

COMPANY: Valentina Oumansky, Anita Grimes, Claudia Morris, Edmund Balin, Amanda Taylor, George Willis

REPERTOIRE (1965-66 Season): "Etudes," "Portrait Of A Young Girl," "A Bow Is A Bow Is A Bow Is A," "Essay For Four Dancers," "Classic Motif," "In The Hills," "The Conductor," "Dance Suite in A Contemporary Mood," "Kaleidoscopemotion," "Conversation In Silence and Sound," "Walls, Corners and Hurdles," "Haikus In Movement," "Lusty Song," "Dance Poem," "The Appel," "The Septagon," "On A Wedding Anniversary."

Albert Duval Photos

Valentina Oumansky in
"A Bow Is A Bow Is A Bow . . ."

Valentina Oumansky in "In The Hills"
Above: "Conversations In Silence And Sound"
Top: Amanda Taylor, Valentina Oumansky,
Claudia Morris, George Willis, Anita Grimes

WESTCHESTER BALLET COMPANY
Ossining, New York

Iris Merrick, Artistic Director and Choreographer; Norman Leyden, Musical Director; Costumes, Sybil Rhodes, Nancy Warren.

PRINCIPAL DANCERS: Sandra Santry, Barry Edson, Janice Rosenthal, Diane Kruppenbacher

COMPANY: Kevin Bernard, Lester Leonard, Frederic Grenot, Leslie Hughes, Valerie Klaus, Honey Laber, Michele Freisen, Sally Andrews, Joan Goldberg, Laura Hays, Susan Crapanzano, Lynn Gandel

REPERTOIRE: "Cinderella," "Little American Serenade," "The Nutcracker Suite," "Les Amour Du Tailleur," "The Fair Of Troubles," "Carousel Pas De Deux," "Masks," "The Bewitched Child," "Caprice," "The Dancing Princesses," "Holiday," "Peter and The Wolf," "Divertissement," "Lighten Mine Eyes . . .," "Patterns," "East Of The Sun . . . West Of The Moon," "The Seasons," "The Secret River," "The Dream Toy Shop," "Ricky," "Thumbelina," and Premieres of "Romeo and Juliet," "Come What May," "Emperor Waltz."

Lucinda Hughes Photos

Sandra Santry, Barry Edson in "Cinderella"

196

Sandra Santry, Barry Edson in "Romeo And Juliet"
Above: Iris Merrick

Frances Alenikoff   Dick Andros   Antonio   Irene Apinee   Gerald Arpino

BIOGRAPHIES

OF DANCERS AND CHOREOGRAPHERS

ADAMS, DIANA. Made professional debut in 1943 in "Oklahoma!." Joined Ballet Theatre in 1944.

AILEY, ALVIN. Born Jan. 5, 1931 in Rogers, Tex. Attended UCLA. Studied with Lester Horton, Hanya Holm, Martha Graham, Anna Sokolow, Karel Shoo, and Charles Weidman. Made debut in 1950 with Lester Horton Dance Theatre, and became choreographer for company in 1953. Made Bdwy bow in 1954 in "House Of Flowers." Formed own company in 1958 and has toured US and abroad.

ALBA, MARIA. Born in China of Spanish-Irish parentage. Began studies in Russian School of Ballet, Peking. Moved to Spain; studied with Regla Ortega, and La Quica. After making professional debut in teens, became one of world's foremost Spanish dancers at 21. Toured with Iglesias Co., and Ballet Espagnol. With Ramon de los Reyes, formed company in 1964 that has toured US, S. America, and Europe.

ALENIKOFF, FRANCES. Studied with Graham, Limon, Horton, Julia Barashkova, Walter Nicks, Mariquita Flores, Syvilla Fort, Martha Melenkoff, Angiola Sartorio, La Meri, Doris Humphrey, Louis Horst, and Anna Sokolow. Began professional career with own solos in Contemporary Dance productions in 1958, shortly thereafter formed own company that has toured annually in US, Canada, and S. America.

ALONSO, ALICIA. Born Alicia Martinez in Havana; married Fernando Alonso. Studied with Federova, and Volkova, and at School of American Ballet. Made debut in musicals. Soloist with Ballet Caravan 1939-40, Ballet Theatre 1941, and in 1948 formed own company in Havana.

ALVAREZ, ANITA. Born in Tyrone, Pa. in 1920. Studied with Martha Graham, and appeared with her company 1936-41. Since 1942 has appeared in Bdwy musicals. Married to George Jacobsen.

ANDROS, DICK. Born in Oklahoma City, March 4, 1926. Trained with San Francisco Ballet, American Theatre Wing, Ballet Arts, Met Ballet, Ballet Theatre, and Ballet Russe. Has appeared with San Francisco Ballet, Irene Hawthorne, Marian Lawrence, John Beggs, Eve Gentry, Greenwich Ballet, Lehigh Valley Ballet, and Dance Originals. Now choreographs and operates own school in Brooklyn.

ANTONIO. Born Antonio Ruiz Soler in 1922 in Seville, Spain. Studied with Realito, Pericet, and Otero. Made professional debut at 7. Became internationally famous with cousin Rosario as "The Kids From Seville." Formed separate companies in 1950's, his becoming Ballets de Madrid. Made NY debut in 1955, and returned in 1964-65.

APINEE, IRENE. Born in Riga, Latvia where she began training at 11. Moved to Canada; founded school in Halifax. Became leading dancer with National Ballet of Canada, and in 1956 became member of Les Ballets Chiriaeff, now called Les Grands Ballets Canadiens. Soloist with Ballet Theatre in 1959. Rejoined Les Grands Ballets in 1965. Married to Gury Gotshalks.

AROVA, SONIA. Born in Sofia, Bulgaria. Studied with Preobrajenska; made debut with Mona Inglesbys International Ballet Co., subsequently appearing with Ballet Rambert, Met Opera Ballet, Petit's Ballet, Tokyo-Kamaki Ballet, Ballet Theatre, Ruth Page Ballet Co.

ARPINO, GERALD. Born on Staten Island, NY. Studied with Mary Ann Wells, May O'Donnell, Gertrude Shurr, and at School of American Ballet. Made debut on Bdwy in "Annie Get Your Gun." Toured with Nana Gollner-Paul Petroff Ballet Russe; became leading male dancer with Joffrey Ballet, and NYC Opera. First choreography was "Ropes" which premiered at YMHA. Currently choreographer and assistant director of Joffrey Ballet.

ASHTON, SIR FREDERICK. Born in Guayaquil, Ecuador, Sept. 17, 1906. Studied with Massine and Marie Rambert. Joined Ida Rubinstein Co. in Paris in 1927, but soon left to join Rambert's Ballet Club for which he choreographed many works, and danced. Charles Cochran engaged him to choreograph for his cabarets. In 1933 was invited to create works for the newly formed Vic Wells Co. and in 1935 joined as dancer and choreographer. Moved with company to Covent Garden, and continued creating some of world's great ballets. Was knighted in 1962; first man so honored for services to ballet. After serving as associate director of Royal Ballet, became its director with the retirement of Dame Ninette de Valois.

ASTAIRE, FRED. Born Frederick Austerlitz in Omaha, Neb. May 10, 1899. Began studying at 5; was in vaudeville with sister Adele at 7; Bdwy debut in 1916 in "Over The Top." Appeared in many musicals and films. Married Phyllis Livingston Potter.

BABILEE, JEAN. Born Jean Gutman in 1923 in Paris. Studied at School of Paris Opera. In 1945 became premier danseur in Les Ballets des Champs-Elysees. Married dancer Natalie Philippart.

| George Balanchine | Valerie Bettis | Erik Bruhn | Robert Blankshine | Lisa Bradley |

BALANCHINE, GEORGE. Born Georges Malitonovitch Balanchivadze in St. Petersburg, Russia on Jan. 22, 1904. Graduate of Imperial School of Ballet. Made debut in 1915 in "Sleeping Beauty." Began choreographing while still in school. Left Russia in 1924 to tour with own company. Became associated with Diaghilev in Paris where he choreographed more than 10 works. Thence to Copenhagen as Ballet Master of Royal Danish Ballet, then joined newly formed Russes de Monte Carlo. Formed Les Ballets in 1933 and toured Europe. Invited to establish school in NY, and in 1934 opened School of American Ballet, followed by American Ballet Co. Choreographed for Met (1935-8), a number of Bdwy musicals, and for such companies as Original Ballet Russe, Sadler's Wells Theatre Ballet, Ballet Russe de Monte Carlo, Ballet Theatre, and Ballet Society. Formed NYC Ballet which premiered in 1948, and since has won international acclaim under his direction. Married to Tanaquil LeClercq.

BARONOVA, IRINA. Born in Petrograd, Russia in 1919. Studied with Olga Preobrajenska. Soloist with Opera; Ballet Russe 1932-40; ballerina with Ballet Theatre 1941-2. More recently has been appearing in plays and musicals.

BARTA, KAROLY. Born in Hungary; made debut there at 11 with local folk ensemble. Studied at Hungarian State Ballet Inst.; performed with Budapest opera and ballet. First choreographic work at 15. Joined Hungarian National Folk Ensemble before emigrating to US in 1957. Attended Met Opera Ballet, and Stone-Camryn School. Joined Chicago Opera Ballet, and continued to choreograph for various groups. Co-founder of Hungarian Ballets Bihari for which he dances and choreographs.

BEATTY, TALLEY. Made professional debut in Bdwy musicals. Joined Ballet Society in 1947. Has more recently toured and given solo performances.

BENTLEY, MURIEL. Born in NYC. Studied with Tomaroff, Tarasoff, Swoboda, Fokine, Ruth St. Denis, Dolin, and at Met Opera School. Made debut with Ruth St. Denis in 1931. Has appeared with Jose Greco 1936-7, at Met 1938-9; joined Ballet Theatre in 1940.

BERIOSOVA, SVETLANA. Born in 1932 in Lithuania. Came to US in 1940; studied at Vilzak-Shollar School. Made debut with Ottawa Ballet Co. in 1947. Appeared with Grand Ballet de Monte Carlo in 1947, and Met Opera in 1948. Joined Sadler's Wells in 1950, and became star ballerina in 1954.

BETTIS, VALERIE. Born in 1920 in Houston, Tex. Studied with Hanya Holm. Made debut with Miss Holm's company in 1937, and as a choreographer in 1941. Subsequently appeared as dancer-choreographer for several Bdwy productions, and own company that toured US and abroad. Teaches in own studio.

BHASKAR. Born Bhaskar Roy Chowdhury in Madras, India, Feb. 11, 1930. Studied with G. Ellappa. Made debut in Madras in 1950 as concert dancer with own company which he brought to NYC in 1956. As dancer and/or choreographer, has appeared on Bdwy and internationally.

BLAIR, DAVID. Born in Yorkshire, Eng. Trained at Royal Ballet School. Subsequently joined its company, rising to rank of principal dancer. Recently honored by Queen Elizabeth with title Commander of the Order of the British Empire.

BLANKSHINE, ROBERT. Born Dec. 22, 1948 in Syracuse, NY. Studied at Am. School of Ballet. Made professional debut in 1965 with Robert Joffrey Ballet Co.

BOLENDER, TODD. Born in Canton, O. Studied with Chester Hale, Vilzak, and at School of Am. Ballet. Soloist with Ballet Caravan in 1937, Littlefield Am. Ballet in 1941; founder-director of Am. Concert Ballet in 1943; joined Ballet Theatre in 1944, Ballet Russe de Monte Carlo in 1945. Did first choreography in 1943. Became dancer-choreographer for Ballet Society, and has continued to choreograph for various companies.

BORIS, RUTHANNA. Born in 1918 in Brooklyn. Studied at Met Opera School, with Helene Veola, and Fokine. Member of Am. Ballet in 1935, Met soloist in 1936, and premiere danseuse 1939-43. Joined Ballet Russe de Monte Carlo in 1943. Has choreographed a number of works.

BOWMAN, PATRICIA. Born in Washington, D.C. Studied with Fokine, Mordkin, Legat, Egorova, and Wallman. Ballerina at Roxy and Radio City Music Hall, with Mordkin Ballet in 1939, Ballet Theatre in 1940, and appeared with Chicago Opera, Fokine Ballet, and in musicals and operettas.

BRADLEY, LISA. Born in Elizabeth, N.J. Studied at Newark Ballet Academy, American Ballet Center, and with Joyce Trisler. Appeared with Garden State Ballet before joining Robert Joffrey Ballet in 1961. Invited to study classic roles with Ulanova. Married to dancer Michael Uthoff.

BRUHN, ERIK. Born Oct. 3, 1928 in Copenhagen, Den. Attended Academie of Royal Danish Theatre, and received training with Royal Danish Ballet with which he made his professional debut in 1947. Became its leading male dancer, and has appeared on tour with the company, and as guest soloist with all leading companies throughout the world, and for brief period was a principal dancer with American Ballet Theatre. Is considered one of world's greatest classical dancers.

BUSTILLO, ZELMA. Born in Cartagena, Colombia, but came to NYC at 6. Graduate of High School of Performing Arts. Appeared with Thalia Mara's Ballet Repertory, at Radio City Music Hall, and with American Festival Ballet before joining Robert Joffrey Ballet Co.

BUTLER, JOHN. Born in Memphis, Tenn., Sept. 29, 1920. Studied with Martha Graham and at American School of Ballet. Made debut with Graham company in 1947. Appeared in Bdwy musicals before becoming choreographer. Formed own company with which he toured.

CAMRYN, WALTER. Born in Helena, Mont. Studied with Bolm, Swoboda, Novikoff, and Stuart. Premier danseur and choreographer for Chicago Civic Opera, Page-Stone Ballet, Federal Theatre Ballet. Director of Stone-Camryn School.

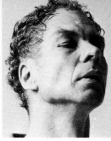
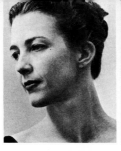

| Dean Crane | Merce Cunningham | Ruth Currier | Alexandra Danilova | Robert Davis |

CARTER, RICHARD. Became principal male dancer of San Francisco Ballet in 1958. With wife, Nancy Johnson, performed in more than fifty countries around the world. Is now director and premier danseur of the San Diego Ballet Co.

CHAMPION, GOWER. Born in Geneva, Ill., June 22, 1920. After appearing in vaudeville, night clubs, and on Bdwy, made debut as choreographer for "Lend An Ear" in 1946. Is now in great demand as choreographer for musicals.

CHASE, LUCIA. Born March 24, 1907 in Waterbury, Conn. Studied at Theatre Guild School, and with Mikhail Mordkin. Became member of his company and danced title role in "Giselle" in 1937. Was principal dancer with Ballet Theatre when it was founded in 1939. In 1945 became co-director with Oliver Smith. Married Thomas Ewing, Jr. who died in 1933. In recent years has appeared only with her company in "Fall River Legend."

CHIRIAEFF, LUDMILLA. Began training at early age in Berlin with Alexandra Nicolaieva. Joined de Basil's Ballets Russe, was soloist with Berlin Opera Ballet, and prima ballerina at Lausanne Municipal Theatre. Opened own academy in Geneva and choreographed for Ballet des Arts, Geneva. Moved to Canada in 1952 and organized own company, ultimately leading to her being founder and artistic director of Les Grands Ballets Canadiens.

CHOUTEAU, YVONNE. Born in Ft. Worth, Tex. in 1929. Studied with Asher, Perkins, Vestoff, Belcher, Bolm, at Vilzak-Shollar School, School of American Ballet. Made dance debut as child in Am. Indian dance company at Chicago's 1933 Fair. Joined Ballet Russe de Monte Carlo in 1943.

CHRISTENSEN, LEW. Born in 1906 in Brigham City, Utah. Studied with uncle Lars Christensen at American School of Ballet. Performer and choreographer since 1934, on Bdwy, for Met Opera, Ballet Caravan, American Ballet Co., and NYC Ballet. In 1938, with brothers Harold and William, founded San Francisco Ballet; has been general director since 1951. Married dancer Gisella Carrialanza.

CHRISTENSEN, WILLIAM. Born Aug. 27, 1902 in Brigham City, Utah. Studied with uncle Lars Christensen, Nascagno, Novikoff, and Fokine. Made debut with Small Ballet Quartet in 1927, subsequently becoming choreographer, ballet master, director and teacher. With brothers Harold and Lew, formed San Francisco Ballet which he directed until 1951 when he established School of Ballet at Un. of Utah. Is director-choreographer for Utah Civic Ballet which he organized in 1963. Married Mignon Lee.

CLOUSER, JAMES. Born in Rochester, NY. Studied at Eastman School of Music. Joined Royal Winnipeg Ballet in 1959, rising to leading dancer, and subsequently choreographing, composing, and designing for the company. In addition to these talents, he is ballet master and assistant director of the company.

COHAN, ROBERT. Soloist with Martha Graham Co. to which he recently returned after 5 years absence, during which opened own school in Boston, joined faculty of Harvard's Drama Center, made solo tours here and abroad, taught in Israel and choreographed for Batsheva Co. there.

COLE, JACK. Began studies and made professional debut with Ted Shawn and His Men Dancers. Has choreographed for and appeared on Bdwy and in Hollywood films.

CONRAD, KAREN. Born in Philadelphia. Made debut with Littlefield Ballet, subsequently appearing with Mordkin Ballet, and Ballet Theatre.

CRANE, DEAN. Born Jan. 5, 1932 in Logan, Iowa. Made professional debut at 14 as aerialist with Pollock Circus. Studied with Nimura, Dokoudovsky, Tudor and Petroff. Became first dancer and choreographer with Ballet Arts Co. Has also appeared on Bdwy and in clubs. Married to actress-dancer Sieglinde Falke.

CRANKO, JOHN. Born in Rustenberg, S. Africa in 1927. Studied at Sadler's Wells. Before becoming choreographer, appeared with Capetown Ballet 1944-5, and Sadler's Wells 1946-7.

CRISTOFORI, JON. Born in Buzzard's Bay, Mass., and began training at 15. Became lead student dancer in National Ballet of Wash., and toured with it until joining Robert Joffrey Ballet.

CUNNINGHAM, MERCE. Born in Centralia, Wash. Studied at Am. School of Ballet. Professional debut as soloist with Martha Graham in 1940; with company through 1945. Began choreographing in 1946; in 1952 formed own company that has toured extensively every year at home and abroad. Teaches in his NYC studio.

CURRIER, RUTH. Born in Ashland, Ohio. Studied with Doris Humphrey and Elsa Kahl. Made debut in 1949 with American Dance Festival. Soloist with Jose Limon Co. 1949-63. Since 1956 has been director-choreographer for own company which has toured US. Also teaches.

D'AMBOISE, JACQUES. Joined NYC Ballet at 15 after 7 years study at School of American Ballet, and rapidly rose to premier danseur. Has frequently appeared in films and on TV, and choreographed "The Chase," "Quatuor," and "Irish Fantasy." Married to former soloist Carolyn George.

DANIELIAN, LEON. Born Oct. 31, 1920 in NYC. Studied with Mordkin and Fokine. Made debut as dancer with Mordkin Ballet in 1937. Has appeared with Original Ballet Russe, Ballet Russe de Monte Carlo, Ballet Theatre, Ballet des Champs Elysees, and San Francisco Ballet. Is now choreographer-director of Ballet de Monte Carlo.

DANILOVA, ALEXANDRA. Born Nov. 20, 1906 in Peterhof, Russia. Graduate of Imperial School of Ballet, and became member of company. Subsequently appeared with Balanchine's company, Les Ballet Russes de Diaghilev, Ballet Russe de Monte Carlo (both de Basil's and Massine's). Made NYC debut in 1948 at Met with Massine's company. Has appeared with and choreographed for NYC Ballet. In 1954 formed and toured with own company The Concert Dance Group. Was choreographer for Met in 1961-62.

DAVIS, ROBERT. Born March 13, 1934 in Durham, N.C. Studied at Wash. School of Ballet, and with Fokine, Franklin, and Joffrey. Made debut in 1960 and has appeared as principal dancer with Washington Ballet, National Ballet of Canada, and Joffrey Ballet. Is also director and choreographer.

| Gemze de Lappe | Katherine Dunham | Louis Falco | Flemming Flindt | Felix Fibich |

de LAPPE, GEMZE. Born Feb. 28, 1922 in Woodhaven, Va. Attended Hunter Coll. and Ballet Arts School. Studied with Duncan, Fokine, Nimura, Caton, and Nemtchinova. Has appeared with Ballet Theatre, and Agnes de Mille Dance Theatre, as well as in several Bdwy productions. Married to John Carisi.

de LAVALLADE, CARMEN. Born March 6, 1931 in Los Angeles. Attended LACC, and studied with Lester Horton. Made professional debut with Horton Dance Theatre, and subsequently toured with the company. Made Bdwy debut in 1954 in "House of Flowers." Has appeared with various companies, including John Butler Co., Met Opera Co., de Lavallade-Ailey Co., Donald McKayle Co., and Ballet Theatre. She is married to Geoffrey Holder.

de MILLE, AGNES. Born in NYC. Graduate of UCLA. Studied with Kosloff, Rambert, Karsavina, Tudor, Sokolova, Caton, Craske, Stroganova, and Dolmetsch. Made debut in 1928 in own dance compositions in U.S. and toured with them in Europe. Became leading choreographer for Bdwy shows. Created first ballet "Black Ritual" for Ballet Theatre in 1940. In 1953 organized Agnes de Mille Dance Theatre which toured the U.S. Besides Bdwy and Ballet Theatre assignments, she has choreographed for Ballet Russe de Monte Carlo, and Royal Winnipeg Ballet. Married to Walter F. Prude, concert manager.

DESTINÉ, JEAN-LÉON. Born in Haiti, March 26, 1928. Attended Howard U. Made professional debut at Jacob's Pillow in 1949. Formed own company and has toured U.S., Europe, and Japan.

DOLIN, ANTON. Born Sydney Francis Patrick Chippendall Healey-Kay in Slinfold, Sussex, Eng. in 1904. Studied with Astafieva, Nijinska. With Diaghileff Company 1921-9, principal dancer with Sadler's Wells 1931-5, Ballet Russe 1939, 1946-8. Founder, director, and dancer with Markova-Dolin Co. 1935-8; 1945; 1947-8. Danced, restaged, and choreographed for Ballet Theatre from inception to 1946. 1949 organized London Festival Ballet. Currently artistic adviser of Les Grands Ballets Canadiens.

DOLLAR, WILLIAM. Born in 1907 in East St. Louis, Mo. Studied with Fokine, Mordkin, Balanchine, Vladimiroff, and Volinine. Lead dancer with Philadelphia Opera, American Ballet 1936-7, Ballet Caravan 1936-8, Ballet Theatre 1940, American Ballet Caravan 1941, New Opera Co. 1942, Ballet International 1944, ballet master for American Concert Ballet 1943, Ballet Society 1946, Grand Ballet de Monte Carlo 1948, and has choreographed many works.

DOUGLAS, SCOTT. Born June 16, 1927 in El Paso, Tex. Appeared with San Francisco Opera Co., John Butler Co., and Ballet Theatre.

DRAPER, PAUL. Born in 1909 in Florence, Italy. Began studies at early age, and became tap soloist, elevating it to ballet-tap concert form. Made debut in 1932 in London. Married to dance soloist Heidi Vosseler.

DUDLEY, JANE. Dancer-choreographer. With Sophie Maslow and William Bales, formed concert Dance Trio.

DUNHAM, KATHERINE. Born June 22, 1912, in Chicago. Debut with Chicago Opera Co. in 1933. Bdwy debut in 1940 in "Cabin In The Sky." Formed own company for which she choreographed; toured with it in 1943, and subsequently in 57 other countries. Is president of Katherine Dunham School of Cultural Arts in NYC which she founded in 1943. Married theatrical designer John T. Pratt.

EGLEVSKY, ANDRE. Born in Moscow in 1917. Received training in France. At 19 joined Rene Blum's Ballet de Monte Carlo. Came to U.S. in 1937, and after appearing with all major companies, joined Ballet Theatre. In 1947 appeared with Grand Ballet du Marquis de Cuevas. In 1950 joined NYC Ballet Co. and danced leading male roles until 1958, also created "Scotch Symphony" and other ballets for the company. In 1955, with his wife, prima ballerina Leda Anchutina, opened ballet school in Massapequa, L.I., and in 1960 formed local classical ballet company which he directs.

ERDMAN, JEAN. Born in Honolulu, Hawaii. Graduate of Sarah Lawrence College. Studied at Bennington, Am. School of Ballet, Hisamatsu School, Martha Graham School, Pukui and Huapala Hawaiian Dance Schools. Made professional dance debut in 1938 with Martha Graham Co., and as a choreographer in 1942. Organized own company in 1950, and made annual U.S. tours through 1960. Made world tour 1963-5 with "The Coach With The Six Insides" which she conceived and staged. Is now head of NYU Dance Dept.

FALCO, LOUIS. Born in NYC; studied with Limon, Weidman, Martha Graham, and at American Ballet Theatre School. Has danced, choreographed, and toured with Jose Limon Co., and choreographed for several other groups.

FALLIS, BARBARA. Born in 1924 in Denver, Colo. Moved to London in 1929. Studied at Mona Clague School, Vic-Wells, and Vilzak-Shollar Schools. Made debut in 1938 in London. Danced with Vic-Wells Ballet 1938-40; joined Ballet Theatre in 1941.

FARRELL, SUZANNE. Began ballet studies in native Cincinnati, subsequently attending School of Am. Ballet. After 15 months was asked to join NYC Ballet, and became a principal dancer in 1965. Balanchine created Dulcinea in "Don Quixote" for her.

FERNANDEZ, ROYES. Born in New Orleans; studied with Lelia Hallers and Vicenzo Celli. Appeared with Ballet Russe, Markova-Dolin Ballet, Ballet Alicia Alonso, de Cuevas' Ballet, before joining Ballet Theatre.

FIBICH, FELIX. Born May 8, 1917 in Warsaw, Poland; attended dance and theatre schools, and made professional debut there in 1936. Became dancer-choreographer in 1939. Formed own company that has toured widely with Israeli and Chassidic dances.

FLINDT, FLEMMING. Entered Danish Royal Ballet School at 10; became member at 18. Invited by Harald Lander to appear in London; returned to Danish Ballet and became leading dancer before joining Paris Opera as danseur etoile, and began to choreograph. Ranks among world's greatest male dancers, and has achieved recognition as choreographer. Became director of Royal Danish Ballet this year.

| Margot Fonteyn | Frederic Franklin | Richard Gain | Eve Gentry | Alexander Grant |

FONAROFF, NINA. Born in NYC in 1914. Studied with Martha Graham, at School of Am. Ballet. Danced with Graham company 1937-46 before forming own company in 1945. Is now teacher-choreographer.

FONTEYN, MARGOT. Born in Surrey, Eng. in 1919. Began training at 14 with Astafieva, and a few months later entered Sadler's Wells School. Made solo debut with its company in 1934 in "The Haunted Ballroom." In 1935, succeeded to ballerina roles of Markova. Unrivalled in dual role of Odette-Odile. Made Dame of British Empire by Queen Elizabeth.

FRANKLIN, FREDERIC. Born in Liverpool, Eng. in 1914. Studied with Legat, Kyasht, and Pruzina. Made debut as child dancer; went to London at 17 to study; appeared in music halls, night clubs, and musicals before joining Markova-Dolin Co. 1935-7. Premier danseur with Ballet Russe de Monte Carlo from 1938; became its ballet master in 1944. Currently director of National Ballet, Wash.

FUENTE, LUIS. Born in Madrid where he began studies at early age. Joined Antonio's Ballets de Madrid and made debut in 1963. Became member of Robert Joffrey Ballet in 1964.

GABLE, CHRISTOPHER. Born in London, and began studies at 11 at Royal Ballet School. At 16 joined Sadler's Wells Opera Ballet, and next year Covent Garden Opera Ballet. In 1957 became member of Royal Ballet where at 19 was advanced to soloist. Married to dancer Carole Needham.

GAIN, RICHARD. Born in Belleville, Ill. Studied with Lalla Baumann, and Martha Graham. Made professional dance debut with St. Louis Municipal Opera, followed by appearances in several musicals. Joined Ballets: USA and danced male leads in "The Cage" and "Afternoon Of A Faun." Became member of Graham Co. in 1961, and also danced with Jazz Ballet Theatre, Lotte Goslar, Sophie Maslow, and Pearl Lang, and formed concert group "Triad" that has performed in NY and on tour. Joined Joffrey Co. in 1964.

GENNARO, PETER. Born in Metairie, La. Studied at Am. Theatre Wing. Dance debut with Chicago San Carlo Opera in 1948, and Bdwy bow same year in "Make Mine Manhattan." After several other musicals and TV, choreographed "Seventh Heaven" in 1955. Is much in demand as dancer and choreographer on television. Married Jean Kinsella.

GENTRY, EVE. Born Aug. 20 in Los Angeles. Used own name Henriette Greenhood until 1945. Studied with Hanya Holm, Martha Graham, Doris Humphrey, Weidman, Tamiris, Barashkova, and at Ballet Arts Studio, and Am. Ballet Center. Made debut with Hanya Holm Co. in NYC and on tour. Since 1949, director-choreographer-soloist with own company.

GIORDANO, GUS. Born July 10, 1930 in St. Louis. Made debut at Roxy Theatre, NYC, in 1948, subsequently appearing in several musicals and on TV before becoming choreographer. Currently director of Giordano Dance Studio in Evanston, Ill., and also of Chicago Company of Dance.

GOLLNER, NANA. Born in Texas. Studied with Kosloff. Soloist with Am. Ballet 1935, de Basil's Ballet Russe 1935-6, Blum's Ballet Russe 1936-7, Ballet Theatre 1939-48. Only American to achieve rank of ballerina in foreign country.

GOPAL, RAM. Hindu dancer, came to U.S. in 1938, and with own company has toured world as its soloist.

GRAHAM, MARTHA. Born in 1902 in Pittsburgh. Studied at Denishawn School of Dance; made debut with its company in 1919, and danced with them until 1923. First choreographed and appeared in NYC in a program of 18 original works in 1926, followed by annual concerts until 1938. A founder of Bennington (Vt.) Dance Festival where she staged several premieres of her works. Formed own company with which she has made numerous successful tours throughout world. Founded Martha Graham School of Contemporary Dance in 1927, and remains its director. Has created over 100 dances.

GRANT, ALEXANDER. Born in Wellington, New Zealand. Entered Sadler's Wells School in 1946, and five months later joined company. Has created more major roles than any other male dancer with Royal Ballet.

GRECO, JOSE. Born Dec. 23, 1919 in Montorio-Nei-Frentani, Compobasso, Italy. Studied with Mme. Veola in NYC, Argentinita and La Quica in Madrid. Made debut as soloist in 1935 with Salmaggi Opera Co. Partner with La Argentinita 1943-4, Pilar Lopez 1946-8, before organizing own company in 1949, with which he has become internationally famous.

GREGORY, CYNTHIA. Born in Los Angeles where she studied with Eva Lorraine, Carmelita Maracci, Michel Panaieff, and Robert Rossellat. Made professional debut with Calif. Children's Ballet. Danced with Santa Monica Civic Ballet, LA Civic Light Opera, and in 1961 joined San Francisco Ballet, and subsequently SF Opera Ballet.

GREY, BERYL. Born in Highgate, Eng. in 1927. Began studies at Sadler's Wells Ballet School, and at 15 danced "Swan Lake" with its company.

HAMILTON, PETER. Born in Trenton, N.J., Sept. 12, 1915. Attended Rutgers. Danced in several Bdwy musicals before becoming choreographer.

HAWKINS, ERICK. Born in Trinidad, Colo. Studied at School of Am. Ballet. Appeared with American Ballet 1934-7, Ballet Caravan 1936-9, and with Martha Graham Co., before becoming choreographer and teacher, and forming own company.

HAYDEN, MELISSA. Born Mildred Herman in Toronto, Can. where she received early training before becoming a charter member of NYC Ballet. Has appeared with National Ballet of Canada, and Royal Ballet. Is in great demand as dance educator and lecture-demonstrator.

HELPMANN, ROBERT. Born April 9, 1909 in Mt. Gambier, Austl. Attended King Alfred College; studied with Laurent Novikov. Made professional debut as dancer in musicals in Austl. In 1933 joined Sadler's Wells (now Royal Ballet) Ballet School, and rose to soloist from 1933-50. Became one of their choreographers, and created the ballet "Hamlet" in 1942. Recently has devoted time to acting and directing.

Hanya Holm

Jillana

Robert Joffrey

Maria Karnilova

Pauline Koner

HIGHTOWER, ROSELLA. Born in 1920 in Ardmore, Okla. Studied at Perkins School of Dance. Appeared with Ballet Russe de Monte Carlo 1938-41, Ballet Theatre 1941-5, Markova-Dolin Co. 1946, Original Ballet Russe 1946-7.

HINKSON, MARY. Born in Philadelphia, March 16, 1930. Graduate of U. of Wisc. Studied with Martha Graham, Louis Horst, Karel Shook, June Taylor, Igor Schwezoff. Made professional debut with Graham Co. in 1952, and still appears as soloist with them. Has also danced with John Butler Co., NYC Opera, and NYC Ballet Co. Married Julien D. Jackson.

HOLDER, GEOFFREY. Born in Port-of-Spain, Trinidad, Aug. 1, 1930. Attended Queens Royal College. First appeared with brother's dance company in Trinidad, later becoming its director. With his company, made first U.S. appearance in 1953. Besides touring, and giving annual concerts with his group, he has appeared on Bdwy, with Met Opera, and John Butler Co.

HOLM, HANYA. Born in Worms-am-Rhine, Ger. Attended Hoch Conserv., Dalcroze Inst., Wigman School of Dance. Made US debut with own company in 1936, followed by annual NY performances and transcontinental tours. Came to US in 1931 to found NY Wigman School of Dance which became her own school in 1936. Has choreographed many musicals and operas both in US and London.

HOVING, LUCAS. Born in Groningen, Holland. Attended Dartington Hall, and Kurt Jooss School. Made professional debut with Kurt Jooss Ballet in 1942. Has appeared with Martha Graham, Jose Limon companies, and with his own. Has also appeared in Bdwy musicals.

HUANG, AL. Born in Shanghai, came to US in 1955. Attended Oregon State U., Perry-Mansfield School, and graduated from UCLA and Bennington. Studied with Carmelita Maracci. Appeared with Lotte Goslar Co. before forming his own, with which he tours when not teaching at UCLA. Married dancer Suzanne Pierce.

JEANMAIRE, RENEE ZIZI. Born in 1924 in Paris. Studied at L'Opera de Paris with Volinine, and with Boris Kniaserf. Made debut with Ballet de Monte Carlo in 1944. Joined Ballets Russes du Colonel de Basil (1945-47), then Roland Petit's Ballets de Paris in 1948. Has also appeared in musicals and films. Married Roland Petit.

JILLANA. After studying from early childhood at School of American Ballet, joined NYC Ballet in early teens, rising rapidly to ballerina. Is active in teaching and touring US.

JOFFREY, ROBERT. Born Dec. 24, 1930 in Seattle, Wash. Began studies at 11 with Mary Ann Wells, later attending School of American Ballet, and studying with May O'Donnell and Gertrude Shurr. Made professional debut as soloist with Roland Petit's Ballets de Paris. Appeared with O'Donnell company, and taught at High School of Performing Arts and Ballet Theatre School before starting his own American Ballet Center in 1950. Formed first company in 1952 that was resident co. of NY Opera, and made tours in his own works in the US and abroad. Reorganized group appeared in 1965 and has been internationally acclaimed.

JOHNSON, NANCY. Studied with Harold and Lew Christensen at San Francisco Ballet School, eventually becoming principal dancer of SF Ballet Co. With husband, Richard Carter, toured world, appearing in fifty nations. Currently prima ballerina with San Diego Ballet Co.

KARNILOVA, MARIA. Born in Hartford, Conn., Aug. 3, 1920. Studied with Michael Mordkin, Michel Fokine, Nenette Charisse, and Margaret Craske. First appeared with Met corps de ballet (1927-34). Became soloist with Ballet Theatre, and Met Opera Ballet. Has appeared recently in several Bdwy musicals. Married to actor George S. Irving.

KAYE, NORA. Born Nora Koreff in NYC in 1920. Studied at Ballet School of Met Opera, and with Michel Fokine. Made debut at 7 with Met's children's corps de ballet. Joined American Ballet Theatre as soloist in 1940 and NYC Ballet in 1950. Married choreographer Herbert Ross.

KEHLET, NIELS. Born in Copenhagen where he began studies at 6, subsequently going to Royal Danish Ballet School. Teachers include Vera Volkova, Stanley Williams, Nora Kiss, and Melissa Hayden. Performed first solo at 16 in Royal Danish Ballet's "Sleeping Beauty." Made concert tour of Africa, and was guest artist with de Cuevas' Ballet, and London Festival Ballet.

KENT, ALLEGRA. Born in Los Angeles where she began her studies. At 13 came to School of American Ballet, and 2 years later joined NYC Ballet. Quickly rose to one of company's leading ballerinas.

KIDD, MICHAEL. Born in NYC Aug. 12, 1919. Attended City College, and School of Am. Ballet. Studied with Blanche Evan, Ludmilla Scholler, Muriel Stewart, and Anatole Vilzak. Appeared as soloist with Ballet Caravan in 1938, and with Eugene Loring Co. Solo dancer with Ballet Theatre (1942-47) before becoming popular choreographer for Bdwy. Married dancer Mary Heater.

KINCH, MYRA. Born in Los Angeles. Graduate of U. of Calif. Solo and concert dancer, and choreographer of satirical ballets.

KING, BRUCE. Born in Oakland, Calif. Graduate of U. of Cal., and NYU. Studied at Hanya Holm, Met Opera Ballet, and Merce Cunningham Schools. Made professional debut in 1950 with Henry St. Playhouse Dance Co. Toured with Merce Cunningham Co., and is choreographer and teacher.

KITCHELL, IVA. Born in Junction City, Kan., March 31, 1912. Appeared with Chicago Opera Ballet before making solo debut as dance satirist in 1940. Has continued as concert artist and teacher.

KOESUN, RUTH ANN. Born May 15, 1928 in Chicago. Studied with Swoboda, Nijinska, Tudor, and Stone-Camryn. Made professional debut with Ballet Theatre in 1946, and is currently one of its principal dancers.

KONER, PAULINE. Born in NYC. Studied with Michel Fokine, Michio Ito, and Angel Cansino. Made solo concert debut in 1930, and has toured in concert and with own company annually since. Has also appeared with Jose Limon, and been successful choreographer and teacher.

| John Kriza | Masami Kuni | Pearl Lang | Judith Lerner | Eugene Loring |

KRASSOVSKA, NATHALIE. Born in Leningrad in 1918. Studied with Preobrajenska, Fokine, Massine, Balanchine, and Nijinska. Prima ballerina with Ballet Russe de Monte Carlo and London Festival Ballet. Currently teaches and dances with Dallas Civic Ballet, and appears with other companies as guest artist.

KRIZA, JOHN. Born Jan. 15, 1919 in Berwyn, Ill. Attended Cicero Jr. Coll., Stone-Camryn School, and studied with Dolin, Vladimeroff, Perejaslavec, Tudor, and Margaret Craske. Danced with WPA Ballet in 1938-9, and joined American Ballet Theatre in 1940, becoming one of its most popular soloists. Is currently its assistant director.

KRUPSKA, DANIA. Born Aug. 13, 1923 in Fall River, Mass. Studied at Ethel Phillips, and Mordkin Ballet Schools. Began dancing at 6 in Europe as Dania Darling. On return to US, joined Catherine Littlefield Ballet. Became member of American Ballet Co. in 1938. More recently has been busy as choreographer. Married to Ted Thurston, actor.

KUNI, MASANI. Started career in Japan at 13. Gained international fame in solo recitals throughout Europe. Graduate of German Dance College, and studied with Mary Wigman and Max Terpis. Has taught and choreographed in Berlin, London, Copenhagen, Italy, Argentina, and Israel. Is currently director of Kuni Inst. of Creative Dance in Tokyo and Los Angeles.

LAING, HUGH. Born in 1911 in Barbados, B.W.I. Studied in London with Craske and Rambert. Long career with Ballet Rambert, and Ballet Theatre, before joining NYC Ballet.

LA MERI. Born Russell Meriwether Hughes in Louisville, Ky., May 13, 1899. Made professional debut in 1928. Made annual tours throughout world until 1957. Established Ethnologic Dance Center and Theater in 1943, which she closed in 1956, and retired in 1960. Has written several books on dance.

LAMHUT, PHYLLIS. Born in NYC where she began her studies at Henry St. Settlement Playhouse. Also studied with Merce Cunningham, and at American Ballet Center. Made professional debut in title role of Nikolais' "Alice In Wonderland" which she performed in NY and on tour. In 1957 gave concert of own works, and has appeared with Murray Louis Co. Married to physicist Albert M. Sutton. In addition to dancing, teaches and choreographs at Henry St. school.

LANDER, TONI. Born in Copenhagen, and studied there with Leif Ornberg, and in School of Royal Danish Ballet. Became member of its company at 17. In 1951 with Harald Lander, who was then her husband, joined Paris Opera Ballet. Later joined London Festival Ballet for 3 years, then Ballet Theatre Francais. Became member of American Ballet Theatre in 1960, and married Bruce Marks, one of its principal dancers.

LANG, HAROLD. Born Dec. 21, 1920 in Daly City, Calif. Made professional debut with SF Opera Co., subsequently dancing with Ballet Russe de Monte Carlo, and Ballet Theatre. More recently has appeared in musicals.

LANG, PEARL. Born May 29 in Chicago. Attended U. of Chicago, and studied at Frances Allis, Martha Graham, American Ballet, Nanette Charisse, and Vicente Celli Schools. Made debut with Ukrainian Folk Dance Co. in 1938, subsequently appearing with Ruth Page, Martha Graham companies before forming her own. Became active choreographer and teacher, and has appeared on Bdwy.

LAYTON, JOE. Born May 3, 1931 in NYC. Studied with Joseph Levinoff. Made Bdwy debut in 1947 as dancer in "Oklahoma!." After many musicals, joined Ballet Ho de George Reich in Paris (1954-5). Returned to NY and has become popular director and choreographer. Married to actress Evelyn Russell.

LEIGH, VICTORIA. Born July 3, 1941 in Brockton, Mass. Studied with Georges Milenoff, and at JoAnna-Imperial Studio. Made professional debut in 1958 with Palm Beach Ballet. Joined American Ballet Theatre in 1961, and became soloist in 1964.

LERNER, JUDITH. Born in Philadelphia, Dec. 30, 1944. Attended Hunter College, American Ballet School, Ballet Theatre School, and studied with Nenette Charisse and Antony Tudor. Made professional debut as soloist with Eglevsky Ballet Co. in 1961, and joined American Ballet Theatre same year.

LICHINE, DAVID. Born in 1910 in Rostov on the Don, Russia. Studied with Egarova, and Nijinska. Joined Ballet Russe, and appeared with Ballet Theatre before becoming choreographer. Married Tatiana Riabouchenska.

LIMON, JOSE. Born in 1908 in Mexico. Studied at Humphrey-Weidman School, and with Tudor. Became soloist before forming own company for which he danced and choreographed.

LINN, BAMBI. Born in Brooklyn, April 26, 1926. Studied with Mikhail Mordkin, Helen Oakes, Hanya Holm, Agnes de Mille, and Helene Platava. Made debut as dancer in 1943 in "Oklahoma!." Subsequently danced with Ballet Theatre, Met Opera ballet, Dance Jubilee Co., and American Ballet Co. Recently returned to Bdwy. Married to Joseph De Juses.

LORING, EUGENE. Born LeRoy Kerpestein in Milwaukee in 1914. Studied at School of Am. Ballet, and with Ballanchine, Muriel Stuart, Anatole Vilzak, and Ludmilla Schollar. Made debut as dancer in 1934 in "Carnival." Subsequently danced with Met Opera Ballet, and Ballet Caravan, for whom he choreographed and starred in "Billy The Kid." Has become a leading choreographer for all mediums. Owns and operates American School of Dance in Hollywood.

LOSCH, TILLY. Born in Vienna, Aust., Nov. 15. Studied ballet with Vienna State Opera, later becoming its premiere danseuse. Toured Europe as dance soloist, and with Harold Kreutzberg. Joined Balanchine Ballets in Paris, and later formed own company "Les Ballets." In addition to choreographing, has appeared on Bdwy.

LOUIS, MURRAY. Born Nov. 4, 1926 in NYC. Graduate of NYU. Studied with Alwin Nikolais, and made professional debut at Henry St. Playhouse in 1953. Has appeared annually since in concerts and on tour with Nikolais, and own company, for which he also choreographs.

Brian MacDonald   Nicholas Magallanes   Alicia Markova   Helen McGehee   Donald McKayle

LUCAS, JONATHAN. Born Aug. 14, 1922 in Sherman, Tex. Graduate of Southern Methodist U. Studied at American Ballet School. First appeared as dancer in 1945 in "A Lady Says Yes," followed by many Bdwy musicals. Became choreographer in 1956.

LUDLOW, CONRAD. Began studies in native San Francisco, and became member of its ballet company where he attained rank of soloist before joining NYC Ballet. Married to former member of company, Joy Feldman.

MacDONALD, BRIAN. Born in Canada where he began choreographing for television. In 1958 became choreographer for Royal Winnipeg Ballet for which he has done 7 ballets, and commutes to Norwegian and Royal Swedish Ballets where he holds position of director at both.

MacLEARY, DONALD. Born in Inverness and trained at Royal Ballet School. Joined company in 1954, became soloist in 1955 and premier danseur in 1959. Has partnered Beriosova on most of her appearances.

MAGALLANES, NICHOLAS. Born in Chihuahua, Mex. Studied at School of Am. Ballet. Danced with Littlefield Ballet, Am. Ballet Caravan, Ballet Russe de Monte Carlo. Principal dancer with NYC Ballet from its inception.

MARCEAU, MARCEL. Born March 22, 1923 in Strasbourg, France. Studied with Charles Dullen and Etienne Decroux. Made professional debut with Barrault-Renaud Co. in 1946. In 1947 formed own company, and among other works, presented "Bip" with whom he has become identified. Subsequently toured Europe, and has made ten tours of US. Married to actress Huguette Malle.

MARCHOWSKY, MARIE. Dancer-choreographer. Studied with Martha Graham; became member of her company 1934-40. With her own company, and as soloist, performing own choreography, has appeared in US and abroad.

MARKOVA, DAME ALICIA. Born Lilian Alice Marks, Dec. 1, 1910. Studied with Seraphine Astafieva and Enrico Cecchetti. Appeared with Diaghilieff Ballet (1925-9), Vic-Wells Ballet (1932-5), Markova-Dolin Ballet (1935-7), Monte Carlo Ballet Russe (1938-41), prima ballerina Ballet Theatre (1941-5), Original Ballet Russe 1946, Markova-Dolin Co. (1947-8), co-founder and prima ballerina London Festival Ballet (1950-2), and has appeared as guest artist with companies throughout the world. Director of Met Opera Ballet since 1963.

MARKS, BRUCE. Born in NYC, and studied at Met Opera School of Ballet with Antony Tudor and Margaret Craske. Joined Met Opera Ballet in 1957, rising to rank of first dancer; joined American Ballet Theatre in 1961 as a principal dancer, and is currently premier danseur with the company. Appeared as guest in 1963 with Royal Swedish Ballet, and in 1965 with London Festival Ballet. Married ballerina Toni Lander.

MARKS, J. Founder of San Francisco Contemporary Dancers Foundation. Has choreographed over 200 works, including award-winning "Caught In The Act" and full-evening "Crime and Punishment." Has written several text books, and taught at Reed College, San Jose State, Duke U., and Minn. and Fla. Universities.

MASSINE, LEONIDE. Born in Moscow, Aug. 9, 1896. Studied at Imperial Ballet School and with Domashoff, Checchetti, and Legat. Discovered by Diaghilev; joined his company in 1914; became principal dancer and choreographer; Ballet de Monte Carlo 1932-41; Ballet National Theatre 1941-4; organized Ballet Russe Highlights 1945-6; subsequently appearing as guest artist and/or choreographer with almost every important company, and in films.

MATTOX, MATT. Born Aug. 18, 1921 in Tulsa, Okla. Attended San Bernardino College; studied with Ernest Belcher, Nico Charisso, Eugene Loring, Louis Da Pron, Evelyn Bruns, Teddy Kerr, and Jack Cole. Made professional debut as dancer in 1946 in "Are You With It?," subsequently appearing in many musicals. Did first choreography in 1958 for "Say, Darling," followed by several Bdwy productions, and Met Opera Ballet.

McBRIDE, PATRICIA. Born in New Jersey, and studied at School of American Ballet. Joined NYC Ballet and attained principal dancer status before leaving teens.

McGEHEE, HELEN. Born in Lynchburg, Va. Honor graduate of Randolph-Macon College. Studied at Martha Graham School, and joined her company. Became first dancer in 1954. Among her choreographic works are "Undine," "Metamorphosis," "Nightmare," "Cassandra," and "Oresteia."

McKAYLE, DONALD. Born in NYC, July 6, 1930. Attended City College; studied at New Dance Group Studio, Martha Graham School, with Nenette Charisse, Karel Shook, and Pearl Primus. Made professional dance debut with New Dance Group Festival in 1948, subsequently appearing with Dudley-Maslow-Bales Co., Jean Erdman Co., NYC Dance Theatre, Anna Sokolow Co., and Martha Graham Co. Formed own company in 1951, and in addition to choreographing, is a teacher. Married to dancer Esta Beck.

McLERIE, ALLYN ANN. Born Dec. 1, 1926 in Grand'Mere, Can. Studied with Nemchinova, Edward Caton, Agnes De Mille, Yudia-Nimura, Hanya Holm, Martha Graham, and Sevilla Forte. First performed in ballet corps of San Carlo Opera Repertoire Co. in 1942. Made Bdwy debut in 1943 in "One Touch Of Venus" followed by many musicals. Married to actor-singer George Gaynes.

MEISTER, HANS. Born in Schaffhausen on the Rhine. Studied at Zurich Opera Ballet School, and with Mme. Rousane. In 1956 joined Royal Ballet School, London. Joined National Ballet of Canada in 1957, and Met Opera Ballet in 1962.

MILLER, BUZZ. Born in 1928 in Snowflake, Ariz. Graduate of Ariz. State College. Made professional dance debut in 1948 in "Magdalena." In addition to a succession of Bdwy musicals, has appeared with Jack Cole Dancers, and Ballets de Paris, and become an active choreographer.

MITCHELL, ARTHUR. Graduate of High School of Performing Arts in his native NY. Studied at School of American Ballet. Joined NYC Ballet in 1955 and rapidly rose to soloist. Was choreographer at Spoleta, Italy Festival for one season.

MITCHELL, JAMES. Born Feb. 29, 1920 in Sacramento, Calif. Graduate of LACC. Made debut as dancer in 1944 in "Bloomer Girl." Joined Ballet Theatre in 1950, subsequently dancing with Met Opera Ballet, Agnes De Mille Dance Theatre, and appearing in several Bdwy productions.

Francisco Moncion   Jack Moore   Mary Ann Niles   Ruth Page   Roland Petit

MONCION, FRANCISCO. Born in Dominican Republic. Studied at School of American Ballet. Danced with New Opera Co., Ballet International, Ballet Russe de Monte Carlo, and Ballet Society which became NYC Ballet. First choreographic work "Pastorale" was performed by company in 1957.

MOORE, JACK. Born March 18, 1926 in Monticello, Ind. Graduate of U. of Iowa. Studied at Martha Graham School, School of American Ballet, Conn. College School of Dance, and Merce Cunningham Studio. Made professional dance debut in 1951, subsequently appearing in companies of Nina Fonaroff, Helen McGehee, Pearl Lang, Katherine Litz, Martha Graham, Anna Sokolow, and City Center Opera Co. Has also appeared in Bdwy musicals, and in his own works annually since 1957. Has taught at Conn. College, Bennington, Juilliard, and UCLA.

MOYLAN, MARY ELLEN. Studied at School of Am. Ballet, and made debut at 16 as leading dancer in operetta "Rosalinda." Following year joined Ballet Russe de Monte Carlo as soloist. In 1950 became ballerina with Ballet Theatre.

MUMAW, BARTON. Born in 1912 in Hazelton, Pa. Studied with Ted Shawn; made professional debut with Shawn's company in 1931 and danced with group until it disbanded. Now makes guest appearances, teaches, and appears in Bdwy musicals, and at Jacob's Pillow.

NAGRIN, DANIEL. Born in NYC, graduate of CCNY. Studied with Martha Graham, Helen Tamiris, Hanya Holm, and Anna Sokolow. Made professional dancing debut in 1945 in "Marianne," followed by several Bdwy musicals, and choreography for Off-Bdwy productions. Married to choreographer-teacher Helen Tamiris.

NAULT, FERNAND. Born Dec. 27, 1921 in Montreal, Can. Studied with Margaret Craske, Antony Tudor, Preobrajenska, Vera Volkova, Pereyslavic, Elizabeth Leese. Made professional debut with American Ballet Theatre in 1944, for which he has been ballet master 20 years. Is artistic director of Louisville Civic Ballet, and associate artistic director of Les Grands Ballets Canadiens, Montreal.

NERINA, NADIA. Born in South Africa where she received her training. Joined Sadler's Wells Ballet, subsequently becoming one of its leading ballerinas.

NIKOLAIS, ALWIN T. Born Nov. 25, 1912 in Southington, Conn. Studied with Martha Graham, Doris Humphrey, Hanya Holm, Louis Horst, John Martin, at Bennington Summer Dance School. Made professional dance debut in 1939. Has choreographed for, and appeared with his own company in the US and abroad. Since 1949 has been co-director of Henry St. Playhouse School of Dance and Theatre.

NILES, MARY ANN. Born May 2, 1933 in NYC. Studied with Nenette Charisse, Ernest Carlos, Frances Cole, and Roye Dodge. Has appeared with American Dance Theatre both in US and Europe. Was half of popular Fosse-Niles Dance Team that toured US and appeared in Bdwy musicals. Currently teaching, dancing, and choreographing.

NILLO, DAVID. Born July 13, 1917 in Goldsboro, N.C. Made debut with Ballet Theatre in 1940, then danced with Ballet Caravan, and Chicago Opera Ballet before appearing in and choreographing several Bdwy musicals.

NIMURA, YEICHI. Born in Suwa, Japan, March 25, 1908. First appeared with Operetta Taza. Soloist Manhattan Opera House 1928. Choreographed for musicals and Met Opera. Currently teaches.

NUREYEV, RUDOLF. Born in 1938 aboard a train in Russia; reared in Tartary, Bashkir. Admitted to Kirov Ballet school at 17; joined its company and became premier danseur. During its 1961 appearance in Paris, he decided to remain. Invited to join Royal Ballet as co-star and partner of Margot Fonteyn. Has recently choreographed several ballets. Considered by many as world's greatest male dancer.

O'DONNELL, MAY. Born in Sacramento, Calif. Made debut with Estelle Reed Concert Group in San Francisco; lead dancer with Martha Graham Co. 1932-44. Formed own school and company for which she dances and choreographs. Married Ray B. Green.

OLRICH, APRIL. Born April Oelrichs in Zanzibar, E. Africa in 1931. Studied with Borovsky, and Tchernicheva. Joined Original Ballet Russe in 1944. Currently appearing on Bdwy in "Wait A Minim."

OSATO, SONO. Born Aug. 29, 1919 in Omaha, Neb. Studied with Egorova, Oboukhoff, Caton, Otto Bolm and Bernice Holmes. Member of corps de ballet and soloist with Ballet Russe de Monte Carlo (1934-40), and with Ballet Theatre (1941-43), followed by several Bdwy musicals, including "One Touch of Venus," "Ballet Ballads," and "Peer Gynt."

OUMANSKY, VALENTINA. Born in Los Angeles; graduate of Mills College. Studied with Alexander Oumansky, Agnes de Mille, Pierre Vladimiroff, Louis Horst, Merce Cunningham, Martha Graham, and Carmelita Maracci. Made professional dance debut with Marquis de Cuevas' Ballet International, subsequently appearing in several Bdwy musicals, before devoting full time to choreography, concert work, and teaching.

PAGE, ANNETTE. Born in Manchester, Eng. Entered Royal Ballet School in 1945, and joined company in 1950. Became ballerina in 1959. Has also toured with Margot Fonteyn, and made guest appearances at Stockholm's Royal Opera.

PAGE, RUTH. Born in Indianapolis, Ind. Studied with Enrico Cecchetti, Adolf Bolm, and Anna Pavlowa. Made professional debut in 1919 with Chicago Opera Co. Toured S. America with Pavlowa, leading dancer in Bdwy's "Music Box Revue," and premiere danseuse with Met Opera. Danced with Diaghileff Ballet Russe, and Ballet Russe de Monte Carlo. Formed own company with Bentley Stone and toured US, Europe, and S. America for 8 years. In Chicago, has been first dancer, choreographer, director for Allied Arts, Grand Opera Co., Federal Theatre, Ravinia Opera Festival. Currently ballet director of both Chicago Opera Ballet and Lyric Opera of Chicago. Married to attorney Thomas H. Fisher.

PETIT, ROLAND. Born in Paris in 1924. Studied at Paris Opera School; became member of corps in 1939, and began choreographing. In 1945 was co-founder, ballet master, choreographer, and premier danseur of Les Ballets des Champs-Elysees. In 1948 formed own company Les Ballets de Paris, for which he dances and choreographs. Married Zizi Jeanmaire.

| Maya Plisetskaya | Jerome Robbins | Rosario | Herbert Ross | Ruth St. Denis |

PLATOFF, MARC. Born Marcel LePlat in Seattle, Wash. in 1915. Made debut with de Basil's Ballet Russe; soloist with Ballet Russe de Monte Carlo 1938-42 and also choreographed for them. As Marc Platt made Bdwy bow in 1943 in "Oklahoma!," subsequently appearing in and choreographing for films. Currently director of Radio City Ballet.

PLISETSKAYA, MAYA. Began studies at Moscow State School of Ballet at 8 and joined Bolshoi company in 1943, rising to premiere danseuse. Internationally famous for her "Swan Lake." Awarded Lenin Prize in 1964. In addition to dancing with Bolshoi, is now teaching. Married composer Rodion Shchedrin.

POWELL, ROBERT. Born in Hawaii, and graduate of High School of Performing Arts. Has been featured dancer with all major American modern dance companies, and appeared for several seasons with NYC Opera Ballet. Currently soloist with Martha Graham Co.

PROKOVSKY, ANDRE. Born in Paris, and achieved recognition in Europe with such companies as Grand Ballet du Marquis de Cuevas and London Festival Ballet, and made world tour with "Stars of The French Ballet." Joined NYC Ballet as principal dancer.

RALL, TOMMY. Born Dec. 27, 1929 in Kansas City, Mo. Attended Chouinard Art Inst. Studied with Carmelita Maracci, David Lichine, and Oboukhoff of School of Am. Ballet. Joined Ballet Theatre in 1944, and became soloist in 1945. Has appeared in Bdwy musicals, and films, and choreographed for TV. Married to actress-singer Monte Amundsen.

RASCH, ALBERTINA. Born in Vienna in 1896. Studied at Royal Opera Ballet School. Made debut in 1909. Was premiere danseuse at NY's Hippodrome (1911), Century Opera House (1913-14), Chicago Opera House (1914-15), Ballet Mistress American Opera Co. (1916). Has choreographed for Bdwy and films. Married to composer Dimitri Tiomkin.

REED, JANET. Born in Tolo, Ore. Studied with William Christensen. Member of San Francisco Ballet 1937-41, Ballet Theatre 1943-6, NYC Ballet.

REYES, RAMON DE LOS. Born in Madrid where he started dancing at 9. Made professional debut at 17 after studying with Antonio Marin. Formed own company that toured Spain, Europe, and US. Joined Ximenez-Vargas Co., and later Roberto Iglesias Co. as leading dancer. With Maria Alba, formed Alba-Reyes Spanish Dance Co. in 1964.

RIABOUCHINSKA, TATIANA. Born May 23, 1916 in Moscow. Studied with Alexandre Volinin, and Mathilda Kchesinska. Made professional debut in London in 1932. Danced with Monte Carlo Ballet Russe de Basil (1933-43), Ballet Theatre, London Festival Ballet, Theatre Colon (Buenos Aires, 1946-47). Has also appeared in Bdwy musicals.

RIVERA, ALONZO. Born Oct. 14, 1936 in Morelia, Michoacan, Mexico. Attended U. of Michoacan. Studied with Sergio Franco, and Leon Escobar, and at Jacob's Pillow. Made professional debut in 1952 and has toured the Americas with Leon Escobar Co. since 1954.

ROBBINS, JEROME. Born Oct. 11, 1918 in NYC. Attended NYU. Studied with Ella Daganova, Platova, Eugene Loring, Antony Tudor, New Dance League, and Helene Veola. Made dance debut in 1937 with Sandor-Sorel Co. Subsequently danced in Bdwy musicals before joining Ballet Theatre in 1940, for which he first choreographed "Fancy Free." Joined NYC Ballet Co. in 1949 and became its associate artistic director in 1950. Formed own company Ballets: U.S.A. which toured Europe and US in 1958, 1959, 1961. Has choreographed and directed many Bdwy productions and ballets.

ROSARIO. Born Rosario Perez in Seville in 1920. Cousin of Antonio with whom she achieved international fame. Studied with Realito. With Antonio, became known as "The Kids From Seville" and toured world together until they separated in 1952. Formed her own ballet company, but changed to dance recitals. Has returned to guest star with Antonio and his Ballets de Madrid.

ROSS, BERTRAM. Leading male dancer of the Martha Graham Co., appears in almost every work in the active repertory. Appeared this season with own company and choreography at YMHA Dance Center. Teaches at Graham School, Juilliard, and Neighborhood Playhouse.

ROSS, HERBERT. Born May 13, 1927 in Brooklyn. Studied with Doris Humphrey, Helene Platova, and Laird Leslie. Made professional debut in 1942-3 touring in Shakespearean repertory company, and dancing debut in "Follow The Girls" in 1944, followed by several other musicals. In 1950 choreographed and appeared with Ballet Theatre in "Caprichos," subsequently choreographing for Bdwy musicals, Met Opera Ballet, American Ballet Theatre, and danced with own company in 1960. Married to ballerina Nora Kaye.

ROSSEN, KEITH. Born in Birmingham, Eng. Studied at Royal Ballet School. Joined Covent Garden Opera Ballet in 1954, and Royal Ballet in 1955. Became soloist in 1959, and principal dancer in 1964.

RUDKO, DORIS. Born Oct. 18, 1919 in Milwaukee. Graduate of U. of Wisc. Studied with Doris Humphrey, Charles Weidman, Jose Limon, Martha Graham, Hanya Holm, Louis Horst, Ella Daganova, Helene Platova, Robert Joffrey, and Nina Fonaroff. Made professional debut on Bdwy in 1946 in "Shootin' Star." Has been concert performer and choreographer since 1947. Formed own company in 1957.

RUIZ, BRUNILDA. Born in Puerto Rico but reared in NYC where she began studies at 12 with Martha Melincoff, and graduated from High School of Performing Arts. Studied with Robert Joffrey before joining his touring group in 1955, and his company in 1961. Also appeared with Philadelphia and NYC Opera companies. Joined Harness Ballet in 1964. Married to dancer-choreographer John Wilson.

SADDLER, DONALD. Born Jan. 24, 1920 in Van Nuys, Calif. Attended LACC. Studied with St. Maracci, Dolin, and Tudor. Made debut in 1937, subsequently appearing with Ballet Theatre (1940-3, 1946-7), and in Bdwy musicals. First choreography "Blue Mountain Ballads" for Markova-Dolin Co. in 1948, followed by other ballets and Bdwy musicals. Performed with own company in 1949. Became assistant artistic director of Harkness Ballet in 1964.

| Paul Sanasardo | Ramon Segarra | Ted Shawn | George Skibine | Mia Slavenska |

ST. DENIS, RUTH. Born in 1877 in Newark, N. J. One of most important pioneers of 20th century American dance, began career in vaudeville and musical comedy before becoming serious dance artist and innovator. Careful study of Hindu philosophy and art led to creation of her ballet "Radha" in 1906. Its success took her on a 3 year European tour. In 1914 met and married Ted Shawn who shared serious, idealistic approach to dance, and together founded Denishawn school which fostered many important figures in modern American dance. The company toured widely in US, and the Orient in 1925-6. Separated from Shawn in 1931 and resumed performing her famous solos, and has devoted herself to furtherance of dance in religion.

SANASARDO, PAUL. Born Sept. 15, 1928 in Chicago. Attended Chicago U. Studied with Antony Tudor, Erika Thimey, Martha Graham, and Mia Slavenska. Made professional dance debut in 1951 with Erika Thimey Dance Theatre. Has appeared with Anna Sokolow, and Pearl Lang companies. In 1958 was founder-director of Studio For Dance, which is school for his own company that has presented concerts throughout the US, Canada, and BWI. Has been choreographer and dancer on TV. Currently Director of Modern Dance Council in Rochester, N.Y.

SHANNE, MARGRETHE. Graduate of Royal Danish Ballet school, and joined its company in mid-1940's, rapidly rising to premiere danseuse and the epitome of the Bournonville style. Briefly joined Petit's Ballets des Champs-Elysees in Paris, and in 1947 made London debut with them before returning to Royal Danish Ballet where she became synonymous with "La Sylphide." Made NY debut in it in 1956, and danced it for her farewell performance this season in NY and Copenhagen. One of the truly great romantic ballerinas is leaving the company for partial retirement.

SCOTT, MARION. July 24, 1922 in Chicago. Studied with Martha Graham, Doris Humphrey, Charles Weidman, Louis Horst, Helen Tamiris, and Mia Slavenska. Made professional debut with Humphrey-Weidman Co. in 1942. Has danced with Tamiris company, and in 1964 formed own company.

SEGARRA, RAMON. Born Nov. 26, 1939 in Mayaguez, P.R. Studied with George Chaffee, Bella Malinka, Lillian Moore, Valentina Pereyaslavec, Anatole Vilzak, Oboukoff, Vladimiroff, Eglevsky, and Hector Zaraspe. Made professional dance debut in 1954 with Ballet Chaffee. subsequently appearing as soloist with May O'Donnell Co. (1956-8), Ballet Russe de Monte Carlo (1958-61), NYC Ballet (1961-4), National Ballet of Canada principal dancer from 1964.

SERRANO, LUPE. Born in Santiago, Chile. Studied in Mexico City with Dambre and joined Mexico City Ballet Co. Organized Mexican Academy of Modern Dance. After studying with Celli and Tudor, performed with Ballet Russe, and Ballet Theatre.

SEYMOUR, LYNN. Born in Wainwright, Alberta, Canada. Besides appearing as dramatic ballerina with Royal Ballet, has made guest appearances with Stuttgart, and Canadian National Ballet.

SHAW, BRIAN. Born in Golcar, Yorkshire, Eng. At 14 joined Sadler's Wells School, and joined company 2 years later, becoming one of Royal Ballet's outstanding principal dancers.

SHAWN, TED. Born in Kansas City, Mo., Oct. 21, 1891, was first male dancer to achieve eminence in US. Attended U. of Denver. Studied with Hazel Wallack, and made professional debut in Denver in 1911. Began next year in Los Angeles to teach, choreograph, and produce. With 4 dancers, began coast-to-coast tour Jan. 1, 1914, during which met and married dancer Ruth St. Denis. Together founded Denishawn school and company which flourished for 17 years, and produced many important contemporary dancers. Made history with tours of America, Europe, and Orient. In 1932, without St. Denis, turned attention to development of male dancers, and in 1933 started what is now the world renowned Jacob's Pillow Dance Festival. With his company of men dancers, toured US, Canada, Cuba, and Eng. until 1940 when selective service seriously curtailed personnel. The Festival is adjunctive to school, The University of The Dance, where students must study ballet, modern, and ethnic dance. In 1957 Shawn was knighted by the King of Denmark. He has also authored many books on the dance.

SHEARER, MOIRA. Born in Dunfermline, Scotland, Jan. 17, 1926. Studied with Legat and Preobrajenska; joined International Ballet at 15, transferring to Sadler's Wells with whom she became ballerina in 1944. More recently has appeared on stage and in films.

SHEARER, SYBIL. Born in Toronto, Can. Studied in France and Eng. Before forming and choreographing for own group, appeared with Humphrey-Weidman Co., and Theatre Dance Co.

SIMONE, KIRSTEN. Born July 1 in Copenhagen. Studied at School of Royal Theatre; made debut with its company in 1952, subsequently becoming principal dancer. Has also appeared with Ruth Page Opera Ballet, Royal Winnipeg Ballet, and Royal Swedish Ballet.

SKIBINE, GEORGE. Born Jan. 17, 1920 in Russia. Studied with Olga Preobrajenska, and Anatol Oboukhoff. Made professional debut with Ballet de Monte Carlo in 1937, and danced with company until 1939. Danced with Original Ballet Russe (1939-40), American Ballet Theatre (1940-1942), Marquis de Cuevas Grand Ballet (1947-56), Theatre National de l'Opera Paris (1956-64), and became artistic director of Harkness Ballet in 1964. Married to ballerina Marjorie Tallchief.

SLAVENSKA, MIA. Born Mia Corak in Yugoslavia. At 12 made debut and toured Europe with Anton Vyanc, subsequently appearing with Lifar and Dolin, and as prima ballerina with Ballet Russe de Monte Carlo, before forming own company Ballet Variant that toured Americas, and Europe. Married Kurt Neumann.

SOKOLOW, ANNA. Born in 1912 in Hartford, Conn. Studied with Martha Graham and Louis Horst. Became member of Graham Co. but left to form own. Has become internationally known as choreographer, and her works include many modern classics. Formed her own Lyric Dance Co. in Israel in 1962. Has taught at major studios and universities, and choreographed for Broadway, TV, and opera.

| Zachary Solov | Marjorie Tallchief | Paul Taylor | Glen Tetley | Clive Thompson |

SOLOV, ZACHARY. Born in Philadelphia. Studied with Catherine Littlefield, Preobrajenska, Ernest Carlos, Hanya Holm, and Doris Humphrey and at American Ballet School. Made first professional appearance with Catherine Littlefield Ballet Co. Later joined American Ballet, New Opera Co., Eugene Loring Dance Players, and Ballet Theatre. In 1951 became choreographer for Met Opera Ballet. Toured with own company during 1961-62. Has also appeared on Bdwy.

SOMES, MICHAEL. Born in Eng.; attended Sadler's Wells School; joined its company in 1937, and became lead dancer in 1938. For many years, partner for Margot Fonteyn, and creator of many famous roles. In 1962 appointed assistant director of company.

SPOHR, ARNOLD. Born in Saskatchewan, Can. Joined Winnepeg company in 1945, rapidly rising to leading dancer, and appeared in England partnering Alicia Markova. Began choreographing for company in 1950. In 1958 was appointed director of Royal Winnipeg Ballet Co. for which he still choreographs.

STACKHOUSE, SALLY. Born in Chicago, graduate of U. of Wisc. Studied with Arrby Blinn, Steffi Nossen, Perry-Mansfield School, John Begg, Jose Limon, Martha Graham, and Daniel Nagrin. Joined Limon company in 1959. Has also appeared with Alvin Ailey Co. Teaches at Juilliard and Conn. College.

STARBUCK, JAMES. Born in Albuquerque, New Mex. Attended College of Pacific. Made dancing debut in 1934 with Ballet Moderne, subsequently appearing with San Francisco Opera Ballet, Ballet Russe de Monte Carlo (1939-44). Danced on Bdwy in several musicals before his first choreography for "Fanny." Has since choreographed and directed many productions for theatre and TV.

STONE, BENTLEY. Born in Plankinston, South Dak. Studied with Severn, Caskey, Albertieri, Novikoff, and Rambert. After dancing in musicals, joined Chicago Civic Opera, becoming premier danseur. Has also danced with Ballet Rambert, Ballet Russe, and Page-Stone Ballet for which he has choreographed many productions.

SVETLOVA, MARINA. Born May 3, 1922 in Paris. Studied with Vera Trefilova, Egorova, and A. Vilzak. Danced with Original Ballet Russe (1939-41), Ballet Theatre (1942), prima ballerina Met Opera Ballet (1943-50), NYC Opera (1950-52), own concert group (1944-58), and as guest with most important European companies. Artistic Director of Dallas Civic Ballet; choreographer for Dallas, Seattle, and Houston Operas.

TALLCHIEF, MARIA. Born Jan. 24, 1925 in Fairfax. Okla. After studying with Bronislava Nijinska, joined Ballet Russe de Monte Carlo in 1942, and became leading dancer. In 1948 joined NYC Ballet as prima ballerina, and excelled in classic roles. Has appeared as guest artist with Paris Opera and other European companies.

TALLCHIEF, MARJORIE. Born on Indian reservation in Oklahoma in 1927. Studied with Bronislava Nijinska, and David Lichine. Made professional debut with American Ballet Theatre in 1945, subsequently appearing with Marquis de Cuevas Ballet (1947-56), Theatre National Opera de Paris (1956-64), Bolshoi (1964), and joined Harkness Ballet in 1964. Married to dancer George Skibine.

TAMIRIS, HELEN. Born Apr. 24, 1905, in NYC. Attended New School of Social Research. Studied at Henry St. Settlement, with Irene Lewison, and Blanche Talmud. Made debut as dancer with Met Opera Ballet in 1921-23, and concert debut as dancer-choreographer in 1925 in "The Music Box Revue," subsequently touring Europe in a solo concert. In 1927 formed School of American Dance, and in 1930 organized her first company with which she toured until 1945. Has choreographed many Bdwy musicals. Since 1960, co-director of Tamiris-Nagrin Co. Married to dancer-choreographer Daniel Nagrin.

TAVERNER, SONIA. Born in England; studied at Sadler's Wells, and joined their company before moving to Canada where she became member of Royal Winnipeg Ballet, developing into its premiere danseuse.

TAYLOR, JUNE. Born in 1918 in Chicago. Studied with Merriel Abbott. Made dancing debut in "George White's Scandals of 1931," subsequently appearing in other musicals. Choreographer for June Taylor Dancers and director of own school.

TAYLOR, PAUL. Born in Allegheny County, Pa., July 29, 1930. Attended Syracuse U., Juilliard, Met Opera Ballet School, and Martha Graham School. Studied with Margaret Craske and Antony Tudor. Was member of Graham Co. for 6 years, and appeared with Merce Cunningham, Pearl Lang, Anna Sokolow, and NYC Ballet. In 1960 formed own company, and toured US and Europe.

TETLEY, GLEN. Born Feb. 3, 1926 in Cleveland, Ohio. Attended Franklin and Marshall College, and NYU graduate. Studied with Hanya Holm, Martha Graham, Antony Tudor, and Margaret Craske. Made professional dance debut in 1946 in "On The Town," subsequently appearing with Hanya Holm (1946-9), John Butler (1951-8), NYC Opera (1951-66), Robert Joffrey (1955-6), Martha Graham (1957-60), American Ballet Theatre (1958-60), Ballets: USA (1960-1), Nederlands Dans Theater (1962-5). Formed own company in 1961. Has also appeared in several Bdwy musicals.

THOMPSON, CLIVE. Born in Kingston, Jamaica, BWI. Studied with, and joined Ivy Baxter's Dance Co. Attended Soohih School of Classical Dance, and University College of West Indies. In 1958 represented Jamaica at Federal Festival of Arts. Won Jamaican award for choreography and contribution to dance. Came to US in 1960, studied with Martha Graham, and joined her company in 1961. Has also appeared with Talley Beatty, Pearl Lang, Yuriko, Geoffrey Holder, and Alvin Ailey. Married to dancer Elizabeth Lauter.

TOMASSON, HELGI. Born in Reykjavik, Iceland. Studied with Sigridur Arman, Erik Bidsted, Vera Volkova, and American Ballet School. Made professional debut in Copenhagen's Pantomime Theatre in 1958. In 1961 joined Robert Joffrey Ballet. In 1964 joined Harkness Ballet. Married to dancer Marlene Rizzo.

TOUMANOVA, TAMARA. Born in 1919. Protege of Pavlowa; danced first leading role with Paris Opera at 10; ballerina with Ballet Russe de Monte Carlo at 16. Joined Rene Blum Co. in 1939; returned to Paris Opera in 1947, and to London with de Cuevas Ballet in 1949. More recently has been making guest appearances. Married Casey Robinson.

Edward Villella	Patricia Wilde	Anne Wilson	Igor Youskevitch	George Zoritch

TUDOR, ANTONY. Born Apr. 4, 1908, in London. Studied with Marie Rambert, and made professional debut with her company in 1930, when he also choreographed his first work. Joined Vic-Wells Ballet (1933-5), and became active choreographer. Formed own company, London Ballet, in NY in 1938. In 1940 joined American Ballet Theatre as soloist and choreographer. Has also produced ballets for NYC Ballet, Teatre Colon, Deutsche Oper, and Komaki Ballet. Was in charge of Met Opera Ballet School (1957-63).

ULANOVA, GALINA. Born in Russia in 1912. Studied with Vagonova. Graduate of Leningrad State School of Ballet. Joined Bolshoi Company and became Russia's greatest lyric ballerina. Now in retirement.

VALENTINE, PAUL. Born William Daixel, March 23, 1919 in NYC. Began career at 14 as dancer with Ballet Russe de Monte Carlo, subsequently as Val Valentinoff danced with Fokine Ballet, and Mordkin Ballet. Since 1937 has appeared in theatre, TV, and night clubs. Married to Princess Flavine Sultana Bashi Abdul Alikhan.

VERDY, VIOLETTE. Born in Brittany, and began professional career at 12. Has appeared with major European ballet companies, including England's Royal Ballet, Petit's Co., and Paris Opera Ballet. Joined NYC Ballet in 1958.

VILLELLA, EDWARD. Began studies at School of American Ballet at 10. Graduate of NYU. Joined NYC Ballet in 1956, and rapidly rose to leading dancer. First male guest artist ever to appear with Royal Danish Ballet. Has appeared in NYC Center productions of "Brigadoon." Is married to dancer Janet Greschler.

VOLLMAR, JOCELYN. Entered San Francisco Ballet School at 12 and joined company at 17. Later performed with NYC Ballet, American Ballet Theatre, de Cuevas Ballet, and Borovansky Australian Ballet. Rejoined SF Ballet in 1957, and has choreographed 2 successful ballets, "Sonnet," "Scherzando."

WALKER, NORMAN. Studied at High School of Performing Arts. Appeared with May O'Donnell, Yuriko, Pauline Koner, and Pearl Lang. Began choreographing while in army, and afterward taught at Utah State U. and choreographed for musicals and festivals throughout US. Now appears with own company, and choreographs for it as well as others, including the Joffrey Co.

WEIDMAN, CHARLES. Born July 22, 1901, in Lincoln, Neb. Studied at Denishawn School of Dance, and with Eleanor Frampton, and Doris Humphrey. Made debut with Martha Graham in "Xochitl." Toured with Denishawn Dancers for 8 years. In 1929, with Doris Humphrey, established their own school and concert company. In 1948, formed own company called "Theatre Dance." Was choreographer for NYC Opera Co., and several Bdwy productions. In 1960, with Mikhail Santoro, established Expression of Two Arts Theatre.

WHITE, FRANKLIN. Born in Shoreham, Kent, Eng. After 3 years with Ballet Rambert, joined Royal Ballet in 1942. Is also well known as lecturer on ballet.

WHITE, ONNA. Born in Nova Scotia. Made professional debut with San Francisco Opera Ballet Co., and Bdwy debut in "Finian's Rainbow." Became assistant choreographer to Michael Kidd, and subsequently choreographer for several Bdwy and London productions. Married to actor-singer Larry Douglas.

WILDE, PATRICIA. Born in Ottawa, Can. in 1928 where she studied before joining Marquis de Cuevas' Ballet International, and continuing studies at School of American Ballet. Joined NYC Ballet in 1950 and has been one of its leading ballerinas ever since, having danced almost every major role in the company's repertoire.

WILSON, ANNE. Born in Philadelphia. Graduate of U. of Chicago. Studied with Fokine, Tudor, Weidman, Elizabeth Anderson, Etienne Decroux, and Heinz Poll. Made professional debut in 1940 with American Ballet Theatre. Has also appeared with Weidman company, and in 1964 formed own group. Noted for solo concert-lecture "The Ballet Story" which she has toured extensively.

WILSON, SALLIE. Born in Ft. Worth, Tex. Studied with Antony Tudor and Margaret Craske. Joined American Ballet Theatre in 1959, and in 1963 was raised to principal dancer. Has also appeared with Met Opera Ballet.

WINTER, ETHEL. Soloist with Martha Graham Co. Has taught Graham Method in various schools in Eng. and appeared as lecture-demonstrator. Her own choreography has received recognition, and is included in repertoire of Batsheva Co. in Israel.

YOUSKEVITCH, IGOR. Born in Yugoslavia in 1912. Studied with Preobrajenska. Made debut in Paris in Nijinska company; joined De Basil's Ballet, then, Ballet Russe de Monte Carlo. In 1946 became premier danseur with Ballet Theatre. Currently operating own school in NYC. Married dancer Anna Scarpova.

YURIKO. Born Feb. 2, 1920 in San Jose, Calif. Began professional career at 6 with group that toured Japan for 7 years. Studied with Martha Graham, and joined her company in 1944, becoming soloist, and choreographer. Formed own company in 1948 with which she has appeared in NY and on tour. Has also appeared in Bdwy musicals. Married to Charles Kikuchi, social worker.

ZORINA, VERA. Born Eva Brigitta Hartwig, Jan. 2, 1917 in Berlin, Ger. Studied with Edwardova, Tatiana and Victor Gsovsky, Dolin, and Legat. Made professional debut in 1930 in Berlin. Toured with Ballet Russe de Monte Carlo (1934-6). Made NYC debut in "I Married An Angel" in 1938. Joined Ballet Theatre in 1943. Subsequently, appeared in several Bdwy productions, and films.

ZORITCH, GEORGE. Born in Moscow in 1919. Studied in Lithuania, Paris, and NY, with Preobrajenska, Vilzak, Vladimiroff, and Oboukhoff. Made professional dance debut in 1933 with Ida Rubenstein Co. in Paris. Joined de Basil Ballet Russe in 1936, Ballet Russe de Monte Carlo in 1938, Grand Ballet du Marquis de Cuevas (1951-8), Marina Svetlova Co. (1961), and currently forming own company for 1966-7 season. Is favorite teacher and choreographer for regional ballet companies.

INDEX

216